Also by Laura Thompson

THE DOGS
A Personal History of Greyhound Racing

Quest for Greatness

A CELEBRATION OF LAMMTARRA
AND THE RACING SEASON

LAURA THOMPSON

MICHAEL JOSEPH
LONDON

MICHAEL JOSEPH LTD

Published by the Penguin Group
27 Wrights Lane, London w8 5tz
Viking Penguin Inc., 375 Hudson Street, New York, New York 10014, USA
Penguin Books Australia Ltd, Ringwood, Victoria, Australia
Penguin Books Canada Ltd, 10 Alcorn Avenue, Toronto, Ontario, Canada m4v 3b2
Penguin Books (NZ) Ltd, 182-190 Wairau Road, Auckland 10, New Zealand

Penguin Books Ltd, Registered Offices: Harmondsworth, Middlesex, England

First published in Great Britain 1996
Copyright © Laura Thompson 1996

Set in 12/15pt Monotype Bembo
Typeset by Datix International Limited, Bungay, Suffolk
Printed in England by Clays Ltd, St Ives plc

A CIP catalogue record for this book is available from the British Library

isbn 0 7181 4159 8

To Lammtarra, a great horse

ACKNOWLEDGEMENTS

I should like to thank the people who gave generously, and un-questioningly, of their time to speak to me: Julia Scott, Frankie Dettori, Walter Swinburn, David Phipps and Geoff Lester.

I am grateful, also, for the invaluable help of Peter Burrell, Dalham Hall Stud, Tom Clarke, editor of *The Sporting Life*, Susan Watt at Michael Joseph, Christopher Little, and my parents, as always.

LIST OF ILLUSTRATIONS

Lammtarra at Moulton Paddocks
Celtic Swing at Angmering Park
Ezzoud loose at Ascot, and winning at Sandown
Pennekamp beats Celtic Swing in the 1995 Two Thousand
    Guineas
Lammtarra's two trainers: Alex Scott and Saeed bin Suroor
Lammtarra and Halling, the star colts at Godolphin
Lammtarra moves through the 1995 Derby field
In the winner's enclosure after the Derby
Lammtarra's Derby jockey, Walter Swinburn
Sheikh Mohammed after the Derby victory
Lammtarra wins the 1995 Derby in record time
Lammtarra winning the 1995 King George VI and Queen
    Elizabeth Diamond Stakes
The Queen with Saeed bin Maktoum Al Maktoum after the
    King George
Frankie's Leap
Lammtarra's victory in the 1995 Prix de l'Arc de Triomphe
Lammtarra at Godolphin

All the photographs in this book are copyright
© Trevor Jones

PROLOGUE

There are moments of magic that come unexpectedly; and there are those that, as you grow to know the rhythms, the desires and some of the mysteries of your life, can be anticipated.

Saturday, 10 June 1995, about 3.30 in the afternoon. The moment of Derby Day when the horses start their slow, staggered emergence into the Epsom paddock. A moment for which my year waits. When it comes, such has been the anticipation that I am unsure what to do with the reality: I simply watch, unblinking, as one of the most beautiful sights on earth unfolds itself beneath the early summer sky.

A couple of these horses are known to me, but most are not. This is essential to the magic of the Derby, that so many secrets lie within these powerful bodies. Of course they have run in the previous year as two-year-olds. They have probably run in the month before the Derby, in competitions of varying prestige; they may even, like the 1995 favourite Pennekamp, have won the Two Thousand Guineas; but still, in the larger scheme of the racing season, they are barely known quantities. They are babies, really. The possibility of greatness glimmers out of their stately movements, and winks at you in the sunlit twitch of their haunches. But it is possibility only. Possibility circles the paddock with the horses, growing as their numbers grow – fifteen of them will finally emerge into this arena – and the start of the race comes nearer. It is an emotion so strong that it seems to suffuse the tight ring, surrounded by the Derby crowd, and blind us to the world beyond; we simply stare, mesmerised, at potential greatness, its light fog criss-crossed by stalking legs.

This is 1995, and the paddock at Epsom is no longer where it used to be, but Nijinsky and Mill Reef are circling it with these barely known horses, and so too are Nashwan and Shergar, The Minstrel and Sir Ivor, Hyperion and Bahram, Persimmon and Ormonde, Gladiateur and Voltigeur, back to the first ever winner of the race, Diomed in 1780 – all of the great Derby winners are walking around the paddock, their shadows drifting among the three-year-olds of 1995. The memory of their greatness is never stronger than at this moment, for this is the moment when greatness like theirs might bloom again. Which of these new young ones might it be? Which of them might become a horse of legend? A horse whose name is exalted in blood lines, in art, in the talk and thoughts of racing people, even – like Nashwan – in the Epsom grandstand bars?

As the race grows nearer, that dreaming haze of possibility takes such a hold upon the paddock that the huge bodies seem to merge into one. Legs criss-crossing like slender branches, coats just beginning to shine in the pale sun, tugging heads, eyes that glance nobly across yours, refusing quite to meet your gaze – that is all that you see in the minute or so before the jockeys strut into the paddock and shift the atmosphere. Earlier I had picked out Pennekamp for my closest study, believing that greatness was most likely to lurk within that purposeful bay frame. I had watched Spectrum, winner of the Irish Two Thousand Guineas, because he carried my money. I had noticed a classically handsome brown colt named Presenting, and a chestnut whose vivid coat seemed at odds with his callow head and shadowy, mournful eye. But now they were all as one. The sound of bookmakers and crowd tension was a distant hum around an intense, oddly grave silence. This moment was over. I walked from the paddock to my seat in the grandstand, and awaited another.

The start of the Derby pierced the air with reality, but then the silence and the fog returned. Nothing in the world but hooves and movement and a tangle of coloured silks. Nothing but my eyes straining slowly around the Epsom course, waiting for the curve to be completed and the emergence into the straight. Nothing but my head inching from left to right, tracing the line of the final three and a half furlongs that take the Derby from Tattenham Corner to the winning post. I was hearing, but not listening to, the commentary on the race. What did I care at this moment, if Spectrum won me twenty pounds? All I cared about was what was going to happen in the Derby.

I had done this before. I knew how good it was, how good it was going to be: a moment of magic that could be anticipated. An inward breath that grows until the body could burst with longing for it to be extended, and yet to be over; a few bare seconds in which time stretches and holds itself while the horses race within it.

What I did not know was that there would be magic here that would come unexpectedly. Two furlongs out, a horse – the dark-eyed chestnut in the paddock – moved sideways from the pack with which he had been inextricably knotted. Then, from a hopeless distance off the pace, he began to run his own race: past one – past two – past five – six – seven, his green and white colours streaming through the air in a blind, bright rush.

Not possible, not possible. Stirred beyond sensation, I said this to myself as he ran without concern, seemingly without hurry. But it kept on being possible. He was coming from another world, another dimension; coming towards the leaders with a bare hundred yards to go and twenty-five still to make up on them; then gliding past them as if, for all its effort, their galloping could no longer take them forwards. The fight of these fine horses meant nothing to him. He had, on the straight at Epsom, become speed incarnate. He had found wings upon his hooves, and in his lungs and heart. His victory had been an impossible one; I had watched, and seen that it could not be done. But I had seen too that it had been inevitable. I had seen Lammtarra put his head down, long and low, and race with his dark eye fixed upon the mystery of greatness.

In Arabic the name means 'invisible', and in a way it is apt. This may seem a strange thing to say about a horse who, during 1995, won not just the Derby, but also the King George VI and Queen Elizabeth Diamond Stakes at Ascot, and the Prix de l'Arc de Triomphe at Longchamp. This is not the Triple Crown, which consists of the Two Thousand Guineas, the Derby and the St Leger; but nowadays Lammtarra's three victories almost certainly have more prestige. They had not been won by a single horse since Mill Reef, himself the first to do so, in 1971. Even Lammtarra's sire, Nijinsky, did not win them all. He won the Triple Crown, but he lost the 1970 Arc by a head.

Yet, for all the magnificence of Lammtarra's record – one which will certainly bring him legendary status and which has caused one of his jockeys, Frankie Dettori, to call him 'the best horse of a generation, and the best I have ever ridden' – throughout his actual career he remained elusive. He came and went, like the spirit of a great horse rather than a horse itself.

At the heart of flat racing, there is an almost painful dialectical pull: between the enduring memory of a horse, and the ephemerality from which the memory proceeds. This dialectic is of the essence, and stronger than in any other sport. In Lammtarra, it found its perfect expression. Never was a sporting career so etiolated and so resonant: it was as thin and fine as one of the horse's own limbs.

Sport will usually paint a picture of greatness over an accumulation of hours and years, using many details, many colours. Yet Lammtarra sketched it in less than ten minutes, with nothing but four clean charcoal lines. During the two seasons in which he raced, he won a minor two-year-old competition, and three of his sport's most prestigious prizes. He did as little as possible, and as much as possible. Nowhere but in flat racing could such a feat be achieved; and even flat racing had never seen anything quite like Lammtarra before.

What he did was beyond compare, so much so that it was almost beyond belief. Watching the horse's victories was like watching Picasso draw them. At the end, there was greatness; but how and when had it happened?

The racing public never quite knew. Lammtarra was always a beat ahead of them. So unexpected was his Derby win that his subsequent triumphs seemed to be achieved before they could be assimilated; it was as if, having been taken initially so much by surprise, those who watched never quite caught up with the horse. By the time they might have been ready to appreciate him, after the Arc, it was too late. Lammtarra was no more than a memory even as his shadow followed his warm, sweating body, covered in its victor's coat, from the paddock at Longchamp.

He had gone back to where he came from: to the protected world of his Arabian owners, and the rarefied world of his Arabian ancestors. His fleeting journey through the racing season was over. He had made it alone, before the watching world could travel on it with him, before even his jockeys really knew where he was taking them; and as he ran towards the greatness that he possessed, he kept its mystery intact.

I

GREATNESS IS WHAT THE sport of flat racing is all about. Handicap races, gambling coups, bravely-achieved third places – these are all a necessary part of its world, but they live in its atmosphere, not at its heart. At its heart lies the quest for greatness.

That is why it is a sport which can alienate. Many people find it too distant, too exalted, too clearly the province of wealth and privilege; as indeed it has to be, since only the truly rich can pursue the purchase of great horses. Of course, that does not mean that other people can't pursue great horses in other ways. They can watch them, gamble on them and follow their progress, but that does not necessarily bring satisfaction. It is too remote a sporting pleasure. Not only are these people trying to form a relationship with a horse that they could never own but also, they sense, with a horse which would shy from the touch of their hand, one whose eye would glance across theirs with the same aloof arrogance as its owner's.

It is so hard to find a way into this sport. Great football teams are owned by rich men, and rich men manage and play for them, but without the spectating masses they are nothing. What would Manchester United be, displaying its multi-million pounds worth of skill and celebrity to a clean, empty Old Trafford? Football needs its crowd, its supporters, and through this need it creates the responding need in the crowd itself. But it is easy, somehow, to imagine flat racing without the response of a crowd. It creates its own hum of noise, its own momentum, its own drama. The greatness of the Derby lies in the race itself, not in the fact that a huge crowd goes to watch it – many people, after all, are there for the day out and not for the racing. If none of them watched those last few furlongs, the magnificence of the Derby would remain undiminished. It would still be what it is: young horses running across the turf towards greatness.

Of course, if race meetings were attended only by those who are closely involved with them, the sport would suffer both financially and atmospherically. Of course flat racing needs its crowds. But – and in this it is different from almost every other sport, especially National Hunt racing – it does not appear to do so. The relationship between spectacle and spectator does not appear to be one of mutual dependency. Perhaps, among other sports, only Formula One racing creates a similar aura of aloofness.

On a lower level, at handicap meetings and small tracks, flat racing inevitably has a homelier air; but the lower level is not really what flat racing is about. A meeting on the all-weather at Lingfield on a winter afternoon is fun, in the way that stock car racing is fun, but again it is peripheral to the heart of flat racing. It is another world. In National Hunt and greyhound racing, there is obviously a similar variation in the quality of the animals; but there is not, somehow, that sense of a complete separation between those who are running towards greatness, and those who are not. At Wolverhampton in late 1995, a name on the card seemed familiar to me but I was unable to place it. It was a shock to read, in the form, that the horse, Maralinga, had run in the Derby that summer. This is not an unusual occurrence, as horses with no chance are frequently entered in the Derby by owners who simply want a runner in the race. But it was clear to me then, as never before, that once a horse has stepped off the path to greatness, it will begin to tread very different roads indeed.

This is not to denigrate the lower level of flat racing. Many people prefer it, for its relative warmth and accessibility, and it is a point of view that I can understand. It is not, however, what flat racing is about. Flat racing is about the horse that might be an earthly Pegasus: breeding it, buying it, understanding it, improving it, perfecting it, riding it to glory. The sport is remote because it is meant to be that way. Indeed, what other way could it be?

I also used to find flat racing too distant. My only contact with it was at big meetings like Royal Ascot which, with their enclosures and badges and dress codes, are a reflection of the sport's rarefied nature. They were social occasions to me, and for a while they were satisfying as such; but to someone who likes sport, and especially animal sport, this eventually became boring. It became unbearable, like perpetual idleness, as I received more and more intimations of the purposeful world within the garden party. When I learned, after several years of attending Royal Ascot, that those four days contain some of the season's best racing, the memory of them drove me mad: I saw myself fiddling with a hat in the Ladies', trying to find the precise and only angle at which its idiocy became elegant, whilst outside drummed the elusive gallop of hooves.

I knew that I would have a better time if I dissociated myself from the crowd that congratulated itself, and attached myself to the far smaller crowd that congratulated the sport. Quite simply, though, I had no idea of how to do it. Read *Timeform*? Interview Henry Cecil? Buy half a fetlock? I knew names and faces and legends, but I knew nothing. Everything was so extreme, so forbidding, so untouchable. It baffled me, all of it: those towering animals with the Dickensian children on their backs, that impenetrable circle of owners and trainers in the centre of the paddock. My father had owned a couple of colts, but their memory converged upon a photograph of a winners' enclosure at an unknown course, with a horse at the centre whose tossing head was no less remote for the fact that my parents' hands had touched him. What was

9

going on? What was it all about? Where was the key to these mysteries?

That key does not exist; or, at least, it turns in the lock only part of the way. Flat racing is a sport that will take you in so far, and no further. I had sensed this, but what I had not realised was that therein lies its magnificence. Its remoteness is not something to resent or to fight against. It is to be accepted, respected, marvelled at. Its mysteries cannot be penetrated, even by those whose wealth or knowledge bring them close to their heart. This is because at their heart stands the finest living racing machine, the thoroughbred horse, and he is a creature that can never be known.

The thoroughbred horse is a true aristocrat. What does that word mean? It means, in its origins, 'the best'; but it has perhaps come to imply something a little more precisely evocative. It implies a separateness, a purity. It implies a connection to past and place that cannot be severed, and that gives an indestructible sense of self. Somehow, too, it implies a sense of destiny. The rugged purposefulness of ancestors may have been softened by time, but something of it still remains, transmuted into smooth and clear certainty within a more aimless modern world.

To apply this definition of an aristocrat to a person is rather a nonsense. When you do so, you are in the parodic world of Royal Ascot and enclosure badges; but when you apply it to a thoroughbred horse, you are in racing's real world. This animal is an aristocrat in a way that a person can never be. When you breed him you know what you are trying to achieve: speed, strength, courage, a will that is his own but that bends to human control. You know what the best, the aristocrat, would be. With a person that could never be possible.

The history of the thoroughbred is therefore quite a simple one. It forms long lines, fretted with the frequent bright ticks of greatness. Every modern thoroughbred is descended, in the male line, from one of three stallions that were brought to England around three hundred years ago, all of whom were named, as was then the custom, after their owners: the Darley Arabian, the Godolphin Arabian and the Byerley Turk. Such is the purity of the racing horse.

Of course there was racing in England before the three Eastern stallions came to the country. The flat, oval Circus Maximus of Ancient Rome, whose vast depression still forms the shape of a course, was replicated in York in the third century. From the Middle Ages onwards, horses were imported to England which bore signs of Arabian blood; James I, who established Newmarket as a centre for hunting (though not for racing – that was done by Charles II) bought an Arabian-type horse called The Markham in 1617.

The three Eastern stallions could not have had the effect that they did, had they been brought into a race of horses without any quality. Certainly there must have been some speed already bred into the English racehorses, possibly from Celtic sources, because Arabians are not especially fast. Markham wrote that 'for swiftness, what nation hath brought forth that horse which hath exceeded the English? When the best Barbaries that ever were in their prime, I saw them overunne by a black Hobbie at Salisbury . . .'

So, though its stock was very few, the thoroughbred must have been evolved to some extent before the three Eastern stallions arrived in England. For example, the fact that around three per cent of modern thoroughbreds are grey can be traced to the influence of two other, earlier Arabian stallions. It is known that some of the mares with which the Byerley, the Godolphin and the Darley were mated bore traces of Arabian blood. Nevertheless, the effect of the three stallions was startling, in both its immediacy and its durability. The Darley in particular caused the breed to take an instant, almost inconceivable, leap forwards; his first generation offspring produced the first great racehorse.

The Byerley was a spoil of war, captured by Captain Byerley in

Turkey in 1686, and later ridden at the Battle of the Boyne. Despite the fact that he covered few mares, his male line can be traced down to powerful dynasties like that of The Tetrarch: foaled in 1911, The Tetrarch looked like a splodgy, rather dirty rocking-horse, but he is thought to be one of the fastest horses that ever ran.

Legend has it that the Godolphin was found pulling a water cart in Paris. The more likely story is that he was foaled in the Yemen in 1724, presented to the King of France and bought by an Englishman, Edward Coke, who later sold him to Lord Godolphin. The 1964 Derby winner, Santa Claus, is a direct descendant.

The Darley came from Aleppo, where Othello slew a Turk and where the finest horses were supposedly bred. He was sent to England by Thomas Darley, British Consul, in 1704. He covered few mares but his son, Flying Childers, was described as 'the fleetest horse that ever ran at Newmarket or, as generally believed, was ever bred in the world'. Flying Childers gave one of the best horses of the day a stone in weight, and, in a race of unspecified distance (probably upwards of two miles), beat him by nearly two furlongs.

One can trace through the Darley Arabian the most powerful bloodline of the late twentieth century: that of Northern Dancer. Foaled in 1961 and by far the most important stallion of the past thirty years, Northern Dancer was the sire of Nijinsky and the grand-sire of Lammtarra.

None of the three Eastern stallions is thought to have raced. Their importance was as progenitors only; they were the best of their kind, and the vital thing about their kind is that it breeds true to type, improving the line of everything with which it mates. You could mate an Arabian with the ugliest old cab horse in the world, and the foal would emerge with some hint of quality. The Arabian is a breed that cannot be destroyed or diminished. It has been fixed in its supremacy by centuries of improvement and reinforcement in the Bedouin desert. Mohammed decreed in the Koran that respect for the Arab horse would be approved by Allah; and this sensible principle has been adhered to ever since.

Paintings of the Byerley and Darley (both by John Wooton) and the Godolphin (by Stubbs) show notable differences between the Eastern horse and the thoroughbred. The paintings seem to exaggerate the Arabian features: the Godolphin, in particular, has a neck whose strong, crested arch begins in the middle of his back, and the heads of all three are as small and delicate as those of china foals. The racehorses of the time wore their tails cropped to a short, stiff brush, which must have made them look very different, in action, from the modern thoroughbred. But the Eastern horses have tails as luxuriant as a young girl's hair, and the Godolphin's hangs almost to the ground.

Next to the Arabian, the thoroughbred looks like what it is: a horse bred to run as fast as possible. The Arabian looks calm, curved and statuesque, the thoroughbred straighter, rangier, alert for movement. The Arabian looks like a horse at ease with the world, the thoroughbred looks ready to run straight through it. There are, inevitably, differences of nature: the thoroughbred is more temperamental, less inherently sound. As a breed it was not named in the General Stud Book until 1821, and the use of Arabian blood in its lines did not stop until some time after this. By the middle of the nineteenth century, the thoroughbred population still numbered only a few thousand. But, in response to the growing popularity of the sport, this figure grew almost continually thereafter. It is impossible to estimate how many thoroughbreds now exist throughout the world, but there are probably about three hundred stallions whose pedigrees make them capable – in theory – of producing a Derby winner.

Yet the number of great horses in the history of the sport remains small. Every season seeks one; but a great horse is not the same thing as the best of the year. For this rarity we should be grateful, because it makes us value these horses as highly as ever. It maintains, too, the links with the past: the names of the greats are strung out like stars, connected by blood and, in more recent years, by the pattern of the racing season.

The recognisable shape of the season began to be formed around the middle of the eighteenth century, when the Jockey Club was founded in Newmarket. The first classic race to be instituted was the St Leger, named after a local sportsman, Lieutenant-Colonel Anthony St Leger, at Doncaster in 1776. In 1779 came the Oaks, named after Lord Derby's house at Epsom; the Derby, first run in 1780, was named after the Earl when he won a toss for the honour against Sir Charles Bunbury. Bunbury, then Steward of the Jockey Club, nonetheless won the first Derby with his horse Diomed. The Two Thousand Guineas was instituted at Newmarket in 1809, with the One Thousand Guineas following in 1814.

The rules governing the classics, that they should be run by three-year-olds, and that the Oaks and the One Thousand Guineas should be for fillies only, have remained unchanged. This has ensured that the attention of the season will always converge upon the three-year-old. A horse will measure itself against these great, classic races; and, accordingly, its own greatness will be measured.

Prior to the institution of the classic races, horses ran over distances which now seem extremely harsh, and without much real regulation of ages and handicapping. Eclipse, for example, a great-great-grandson of the Darley Arabian, did not race until he was five. When he did so, in 1769, it was at Epsom in a £50 Plate, run from the Oaks house to the Downs in three four-mile heats. It was after the first of these heats that an Irish gambler, asked to predict the result of the second heat, said it would be 'Eclipse first – the rest nowhere.' Eclipse did indeed win the race by more than two hundred yards, and throughout his career of eighteen runs was always similarly clear of the field. Freakish supremacy of this kind occurred periodically in the earlier years of the thoroughbred. Presumably this is partly due to the fact that the sport was then less intensely regulated; also that the breed was still evolving, moving forwards by strange, miraculous leaps that would, almost certainly, be impossible today.

Yet the mysteries of thoroughbred greatness are no less impenetrable today than they were two hundred years ago. Of course, anyone with enough money to buy an Oaks winner could mate her to a Derby winner, then wait for the offspring to win one of the same two races. Of course this is a more likely strategy than mating a Group Three winner to the runner-up in a big handicap. Of course Lammtarra was the son of the 1970 Derby winner – Nijinsky – and the 1989 Oaks winner – Snow Bride (promoted to first after the disqualification of the Aga Khan's Aliysa). But greatness is still a very different thing from ability. Ability can be predicted. Greatness cannot. It can only be intuited.

St Simon, for example, was probably the greatest horse of the late nineteenth century. Again, he was a descendant of the Darley Arabian. He was, too, the son of a Derby winner, though out of a relatively undistinguished mare. It could be expected that he would be a good horse. But St Simon was a freak, a force of nature, a horse of whom his Newmarket trainer, Matthew Dawson – one of the most successful of all time – said: 'I have trained only one smashing good horse in my life: St Simon.' He had, Dawson said, an 'electricity' about him, even in the way that he moved about his box, and ran as if 'made of elastic'.

Looking at a picture of the horse, you can see that he was a devil, with an arrogant eye that threatens thunder; the stable hand holding him by the rein looks numb with fear at what he might do next. Indeed, several lads left Dawson's yard rather than attempt to groom him. One of those who stayed said – and one can imagine what he meant – that it was all very well to talk about the patience of Job, but Job had never had to groom St Simon. The only thing that could straighten, temporarily, the kink in his nature was to come at him with an umbrella. Stable hands grew adept at improvising with sticks and bowler hats; rather like Van Helsing crossing two bits of firewood in front of Dracula.

St Simon had been sold to the Duke of Portland for sixteen hundred guineas – a vast sum – when his original owner, Prince Batthyany, dropped dead on Newmarket racecourse, overcome by the prospect of watching one of his horses run the Two Thousand Guineas. Because of this, St Simon's place was voided in the races for which the Prince had entered him. He contested none of the classics, which makes his reputation all the more remarkable. It depends chiefly on his running of the Gold Cup at Ascot, a two-and-a-half mile race, now run only by horses that are specifically bred to stay the distance. St Simon had already won much shorter races with ridiculous ease and with no preparation. For the Gold Cup, Dawson did decide to prepare him; he won the race by twenty lengths, but was only just getting into his stride by then, and his jockey was unable to pull him up until he had made another full circuit of the course.

How could such a horse be fathomed? Even Matthew Dawson, who must have known more about him than anyone did, was finally unable to comprehend what went on inside that huge, prancing body. The journey towards the heart of a thoroughbred is a fascinating one. Everything that they do will tell you more about their nature, their running, the ground that they like, the distance that they want, the jockey who will work best with them. But it is a journey that will take you so far, and no further.

Almost one hundred years after the death of St Simon, the larger number of fine thoroughbreds capable of breeding their own kind have, to some extent, levelled out the standards of the sport. But the great horse is still St Simon's descendant, and that of Flying Childers and Eclipse – literally so in the case of Lammtarra. He could not fly from the rest of the field as his ancestors had done. They ran with him, though, down his short road to greatness, their shadowy bodies guarding the mystery of their kind.

★

The dancer Nijinsky said of himself that when he died, he would be reincarnated as a stallion. His gift was so supreme, so unfathomable, that it could not be compared with that of a human being: only with that of an animal. Perhaps that is true of all the most powerful physical talents. Certainly, the athletes that compel me most strongly are those who have about them something that seems beyond the human and the known.

We are told all the time that what we want from sport is a *connection*. We want to be able to identify with what we see; we want to feel affection for it; we want its repetitiveness, its familiarity, its warmth around us. We want to belong to it, and it to belong to us. We want to see, therefore, those sporting stars who, for all their talent and success, have something in them to which we can relate: in which we see ourselves.

Of course this is true. It may sound like a contradiction, but that is why so many people love National Hunt racing: because in it the horses become like human beings, like us. Their careers last so long by comparison with flat racers – perhaps four times as long – that their audience feels itself to share in the intimate knowledge of the horses' connections. Here there is none of that pull between enduring memory and ephemeral reality. Jump horses can, at their best, win the same races over and over again, as Red Rum did with the Grand National and Desert Orchid with the King George VI Chase.

The races that they win could scarcely be more different from the great races of the flat: they are long, hard, grinding treks, not elegant curves swept by speed. A National Hunt race is one in which you will watch a great horse find itself, unearthing ever-deeper reserves of courage and will, conquering fatigue with each triumphant leap. It is hard not to be moved by the sight of such a horse slowly running the last flat yards to the post, ears pricked with understanding of what he has done, exhausted head proudly alert to the answering knowledge of the crowd.

These are races within which relationships are formed, between spectacle and spectator, that run deep with love. The fact that I hate National Hunt — this love is won at too high a price in beautiful broken necks and legs snapped like frosted twigs — does not mean that I can't see the joy of it. I too loved Red Rum and Desert Orchid: the wisdom in their mature horse heads, the knowledge in their brave horse bodies. I see the miracle of identification with these animals. They are, after all, human beings with all the bad stuff left out.

The greatness of a National Hunt horse is not, however, an absolute thing: it is a greatness of heart and of will, but it is not pure, pure greatness. And pure greatness is the other side of what we — or at least I — want from sport. I want St Simon and Eclipse, running away from the field because they are able to do so. I want Lammtarra, streaming through the Derby horses because he suddenly discovered that he could. I want Nijinsky, reincarnated as a stallion. I want something with which I *cannot* identify, something beyond myself, something whose eyes look into a place that I can't see. I want that dimension of awe which perhaps only flat racing, amongst sports, possesses.

It is the only sport which does not, by its nature, create or require allegiance. Allegiance is innate in human sport: how could you have football, or rugby, or cricket, or even athletics, without it? Spectators are, almost by definition, supporters. They have their team, or their club, or their country; they identify their fate with them; they *care* about them. A bad game is a good game if the right team wins.

National Hunt and greyhound racing do not, of course, supply automatic allegiance. But because they are accessible, and because it is not necessary to be a millionaire to own a steeplechaser or a dog, allegiance is somehow a part of them: amongst their crowds will be those who own these animals, and these owners will be a *part* of those crowds. They will not be remote. They will be in the miasma of the meeting, their ears open to the raw shouts of bookmakers, their noses unprotected from the dirty smell of smoke and beer and hot dogs. They will not live within the scented dusk of boxes and enclosures and wealth's warm cloak; they will not move through a different, sharper, more direct world.

In flat racing, the mass of the crowd is separate from that inner world. Allegiance, therefore, does not come naturally, for the simple reason that it is not necessary. The sport can do without it. Of course, there is a gambler's allegiance to the horse that he has backed, but that is a different thing. And there have, of course, been horses who have commanded the will of the crowd to see them win: Nijinsky, when he ran in the Prix de l'Arc de Triomphe, was such a horse, as was Mill Reef, who was a gentleman as well as a great champion. In 1995, the collective will of the racing public converged upon one horse, Celtic Swing, with a force that, strengthened as it was by the power of the media, has perhaps never before been felt by the sport. But this is not the natural state of affairs in flat racing. The natural race is the one that is run, almost within a vacuum, by horses who move within their own mysterious and magical world.

Perhaps this explains why, amongst the followers that I know of football, or rugby, or cricket, few of them care for flat racing. They might have a bet on the Grand National, they might even have backed Piggott in the occasional Derby, but they have not heard of Lammtarra. Why should they take an interest in such a horse? He does not need them. He is too separate, too protected, too perfect.

Nor, in fact, did a large proportion of the racing public care much for Lammtarra, with his cool-eyed elusiveness. These people, too, prefer the champion with whom there is a possibility of identification: the expected one, the one whose victory has been dreamed already, in whom an emotional investment has already been made. This is understandable, of course. Whose heart would not, a quarter of a century ago, have swelled to the sight of Nijinsky winning the Arc, bringing the racing season to its rightful conclusion, making of it a satisfying and unbearably moving drama? Whose heart did not swell when Mill Reef won the race in the following year and, somehow, made everything all right by doing so?

But those who truly love flat racing – for what it is, not for what they would like it to be – accept, I think, that such glorious autumn days are a rare gift from the sport. Perhaps two or three times in a season, perhaps less often, the race will be run as the public wants it to be. In 1995, it happened when a nine-year-old grey, Further Flight, won the Jockey Club Cup at Newmarket for the fifth successive year, and the crowd around the winners' enclosure wept as he was led in. This was a beautiful moment: one in which the racing public united to show its appreciation of a brave and lovely horse. Far more often, though, during 1995, the public was thwarted in its desires. Events simply took any hope of allegiance away from it. Frustrating though this can be, those who truly love flat racing understand that this is, nonetheless, the way that things are meant to be.

Flat racing concerns itself with something beyond the familiar sporting world of allegiance. It concerns itself with pure victory: with greatness. And when one thinks of the memories that even human sport has decreed most precious – of George Best, teasing a ball past men whose feet had suddenly become leaden and hopeless, or of Brian Lara guiding his bat towards a smiling sun, or of Muhammad Ali, dancing round the ring like a playful young god – one realises that the quest for greatness is, after all, the other side of what we want from sport.

And what greater athlete can there be than the thoroughbred horse? There is no better racer on earth. Nothing on earth can produce such a speed, and still allow itself to be harnessed; for, although the thoroughbred is a separate and mysterious creature, it is only through its relationship with man that it becomes a racehorse. It is only through the pull between horse and man that flat racing becomes sport. Here you have a force of nature, an animal bred to run as fast as possible; here you have those who can harness that force. Greatness is not, in any sphere, a wholly natural thing. It is nature in symphony with effort: in this case, the horse in partnership with man.

There seems to me a dignity in this relationship, again because it is so pure and so extreme. At its worst, man simply uses the horse for his own selfish ends. At its best, though, it ennobles both horse and man. Man is afforded the privilege of handling all that warm, wayward and powerful life; the horse is maintained as an aristocrat amongst animals and athletes. The dignity of this relationship is felt most strongly, of course, by those people who deal directly with the horse – jockey, trainer, breeder. It can communicate itself, however, to those who observe it – the spectators. The crowd may not feel needed by flat racing. It may not always feel able to identify with these huge, alien, impossibly expensive creatures. But it is, if it allows itself to be, dignified by them.

Certainly I feel dignity in my relationship with flat racing. I feel a respect for it which can, as I watch, translate itself into a strange desire: to be as noble and purposeful as a thoroughbred horse, to be an aristocrat as he is. Sometimes, for a fleeting and fantastical moment, as for example when I travelled the final yards of Epsom with Lammtarra, that desire seems to come true, and I seem to penetrate the mystery of greatness. The fact that this is the most perfect of illusions does not stop it from being, at the same time, a perfect moment.

II

E ZZOUD WAS NOT A great horse. He was – what shall I say? – a fine horse. But he was the St Simon of his day; and in 1994 I fell in love with him just as in 1884 I would, I think, have fallen in love with St Simon. He was the start of it all for me.

Falling in love, rather than loving, is the appropriate phrase. The brief magnificence with which flat racehorses erupt into the season, the sense that at any moment they might withdraw from it, makes them creatures with which one does fall in love, in a sudden and violent way. Even when the emotion endures, as it does with horses that live a long while on the turf or in the memory, and deepens into something more like love itself, it retains that first quickening spark.

My feelings for Ezzoud were entirely comparable with those of falling in love with a person. The sight of him opened up in me a kind of delicious alarm, quickly filled by a mixture of terror, tenderness and awe. I would have given a great deal to touch him, but the consequences of this touch would have been something for which neither he nor I could answer. If Ezzoud was not as great a horse as St Simon, equally he was not as badly-behaved. Like him, however, he was remorseless in his demands for respect and alertness; like him, he had a mind of his own whose whims and passions were simply beyond comprehension.

I first came upon him in July 1994, the last year of his career, when he ran in the Coral-Eclipse Stakes at Sandown. This is the first Group One race of the season open to horses of all ages; Ezzoud was then five, and he was running against Erhaab, the winner of the Derby and favourite for the race.

I was watching the Coral-Eclipse Stakes because, the month before, I had seen Erhaab. I had gone to Epsom for the Derby and seen the smooth explosion of acceleration as, his coat black and oily in the sun, the brave little horse moved through the final furlongs and won a victory almost as spectacular as Lammtarra's. Subsequently, there was doubt about how many of the horses passed by Erhaab had actually stayed a mile and a half – had he been sprinting, with full lungs, away from horses with nothing left to give? – but the romance of his victory was such that, at the moment of his doing it, thoughts of that kind were not in my head. Nor did I particularly want to think them afterwards. I was ready, with the running of the Coral-Eclipse, to find proof of Erhaab's greatness.

Despite the disadvantage of his age – the race comes early in the season, and Erhaab, a late foal, was barely more than three – he was odds-on for the race. Two furlongs out, however, an unknown horse in blinkers, with a peculiar and uncommitted action, ran past him. Yearning as I had been for the Derby form to be confirmed in all its magic, I was resentful of this blinkered animal, this Ezzoud, with his five-year-old's strength and invisible eyes. Three weeks later, however, I was to fall in love with him. It was a perverse reaction to perverse behaviour.

I was watching on television the King George VI and Queen Elizabeth Diamond Stakes at Ascot; like the Coral-Eclipse, it is a race for all ages, but with considerably greater prestige. This was the first time that I can recall giving a televised race my absolute attention. I had grown up in a house in which, every Saturday, the afternoon was punctuated by the sounds of racing: the measured, conversational assessments as the horses circled the paddock; the

23

quicker, more businesslike relaying of movements in the betting market; the tense ellipses between the entry of each horse into the starting stalls; and then, through the crescendoing roar of the crowd, Peter O'Sullevan's steady climb through the diatonic scale. My attention would, on occasions, be compelled by a sudden rustle of my father's *Sporting Life*, and a suppressed jerk of the head as a certain horse moved to the front; then the rest of the family would exchange a glance which said that we knew he had had a bet. Sometimes I would simply gaze, without thought, at the beauty of the animals within the summer sun. Almost always I would watch the last furlong of a race, fascinated by the moment in which the blur of brightness and movement clarified, then separated to form its final, inevitable shape.

But never, until the King George of 1994, do I remember sitting down in front of the television with the specific purpose of watching an entire horse race. Then, though, I actually knew two of the horses that were running in it: Erhaab and Ezzoud. Somehow, knowing two was more than twice as significant as knowing one. It gave to the race a history, a depth, a pattern.

I think that I was still hoping for victory for Erhaab but, before the race had even started, I became fascinated by the antics of Ezzoud. He was prancing in circles behind the stalls, his head in its executioner's hood rearing and jerking. Walter Swinburn, on his back, looked unusually pale and small. Eventually Ezzoud entered the stalls, where he stood with a rather dangerous look about him, his eyes bulging like those of a magnified insect. Within perhaps a second of the gates opening, he had thrown Swinburn to the ground, and begun to run the race in the way that he had always intended: on his own.

My respect for the King George VI and Queen Elizabeth Diamond Stakes is huge, but at that moment my respect for Ezzoud was greater. Had the race been disrupted by anything other than one of its competitors – a drunk, say, as had happened that year at

Royal Ascot – I should have been disgusted. Had I had a horse in the race, I should have been devastated. Had Ezzoud damaged either himself or any other horse, I should have been distraught. Had I been the bruised Walter Swinburn, I should have been downright bloody furious. None of these things being the case, however, I began to find the whole thing profoundly comic.

For Ezzoud was, in his way, running the race properly. Glinting demoniacally, his masked head bobbed alongside the other horses as he galloped in step with them. He was where he wanted to be, with the pack, and doing what he wanted to do: telling it who was boss. My heart swelled with love as he refused to do the decent thing and get out of everyone's way.

In the home straight his progress became rather more wayward; perhaps the quickening pace had made him more agitated and feisty. He began to perform a kind of serpentine through the course and, showing no favours, hampered almost every leading horse in turn. Erhaab, whose unlucky charm Ezzoud seemed to be, suffered especially badly; and the one horse who managed to stick to his run, King's Theatre, did in fact win the race. 'And it's King's Theatre!' sang Peter O'Sullevan, resolutely ignoring the fact that Ezzoud, now running a proper race again, had beaten him to the line by a couple of lengths.

Probably King's Theatre would have won anyway, for he was always travelling well; though, after his second place in the Derby, there had been doubt about his ability truly to stay a mile and a half. And it would be hard, certainly, to say that the placings of the rest of the field had not been affected.

It was a travesty, but it was magnificent. The sight of Ezzoud's head bobbing down the course, inducing around it a kind of enthralled fear, seemed to say that flat racing, for all its wealth and prestige and organisation, could be made ridiculous in a second by the impulse of a horse. Remember, it said, to respect the horse above all else.

25

I would have remained fascinated by Ezzoud even if his career had ended then, but, like all the most fascinating love objects, he was capable of asserting his individuality in ways that could not be predicted. Having been bad, he was about to be good. Having reminded us of the need to respect him, he was about to show us why such respect was deserved.

Three weeks after the King George, he won the Group One Juddmonte International Stakes at York, and became only the second horse to do so in successive years. Not just that, he won it in the manner of the most guileless horse alive. His preference had always been to come for the lead as late as possible, with, as it were, a target at which to hurl himself. However, the peculiarly paceless running of the race forced Walter Swinburn – who had come out of the stalls with both hands clutching Ezzoud's mane – to commit the horse two furlongs out, and from there he fought all the way. His masked head bobbed fiercely against the open one of Muhtarram, straining and battling and sticking out the neck by which he was to win: 'He's in a going mood today,' said the commentator. Perhaps he enjoyed it. Certainly, that day, no horse in the world wanted victory more than he did.

After this, he ran in the Arc. The race card, which knew what it was talking about, described him as an 'excellent cheval britan-nique'; but, as it also said, the mile-and-a-half distance was one at which he 'n'a jamais brillé'. He finished a fine fourth, and after a last race in the USA Breeders' Cup was retired to stud. It would be a brave breeder who mated a mare to him, but those who dared might be rewarded in the most surprising and wonderful ways.

Erhaab had put the key in the lock, and Ezzoud had started, irresist-ibly, to turn it. Through them understanding of this sport began to glimmer. I had realised the most important thing of all: that the mysteries of the thoroughbred are at its heart. Trying to fathom them is, throughout the season, a pleasure of infinite fascination and delight. Knowing that, ultimately, they are unfathomable, brings an even deeper joy.

Ezzoud was not a great horse in his running, but he showed more clearly than any other the quality that I admire most in horses, the one that is at the centre of their greatness. He was his own man. Abundant with talent, miserly in its deployment; hugely frustrating, proportionately rewarding. 'Not straightforward,' as Walter Swinburn, delicately understating the case, said of him, 'but brilliant.'

Amid all those noble brows, his slit-eyed mask looked like a badge of disgrace, as indeed in a way it was. His ears stuck through it like smooth, curving spikes. When it came off his eye gleamed wildly, faintly contemptuous and not a little sadistic: he knew that he had his followers horribly hooked. His heart was not quite in the right place – often he kept his brain there instead – but, when he wanted to be, he was almost great. Had he been great, I suppose I would have adored him all the more, because greatness is of the essence here; a win in the Arc would have intensified, to an almost unbearable degree, the feelings that I already had about him. But he was great enough, in his way, as he was. I shall always be grateful to him.

Before him, all I had really known of individual horses was names. Names, of course, have their own power, especially in sport: think of the totemic significance that has attached itself to the Classified Football Results. Merely to hear the sound of the words Nijinsky, Mill Reef, Brigadier Gerard – names from my childhood, as these things so often are – would conjure a splendid thundery sky in my head. That sky still forms when I think about flat racing, even when I think about Lammtarra, of whom I know a great deal. If it didn't, I would know that the power of the sport had waned for me.

That is something that I can't imagine happening, because with its dimension of awe it has something that no other sport possesses, something more akin to art. When I thought, after watching Ezzoud's triumph in the Juddmonte International, of all that was to

27

be discovered in the 1995 season – so many races, so many horses, so much to learn and worship – I felt as if I had just read my first line of Dostoevsky, or first looked at a Van Gogh. All sport has a potentially transcendent quality about it. Flat racing seemed to me to have this quality in its very bones.

After Ezzoud's run in the Arc, my thoughts of the following season were solipsistic and dreamy. He would be gone, but there would be others, of course, capable of compelling the emotions, even if they could not do so with quite his wicked panache. Who these horses would be, I had no idea at all. Obviously, I thought, there would be two-year-olds running then who would command the great races of 1995. But I was forming no expectations, just waiting, willing to accept whatever the new season would give to me. On 22 October 1994, that was all to change.

Throughout the summer, while my eyes had been fixed upon Ezzoud, things had been happening elsewhere. On 16 July, for example, two weeks after the Coral-Eclipse had first brought the horse to my attention, there was an evening meeting at Ayr. The 8.20 was a seven furlong maiden race for two-year-olds. Odds-on favourite was a horse called Chilly Billy, who subsequently won an important two-year-old race, the Gimcrack Stakes at York. However, the Ayr race was won with ease by the 7–2 shot, a novice horse named Celtic Swing.

On 12 August, five days before Ezzoud's victory in the Juddmonte International, a race was run at Newbury called the Washington Singer Stakes. Won in 1991 by subsequent Two Thousand Guineas winner, Rodrigo de Triano, this was a listed competition for two-year-olds. It was, therefore, somewhat more prestigious than the Ayr race, though the prize money was less than £9,000. Again, it was run over seven furlongs; again, there was a short-priced favourite.

The record of Myself stood out clearly from that of the rest of the field, two of whom had never run before. A handsome daughter of Nashwan, she had finished a close second in the Queen Mary Stakes at Royal Ascot, a race that is one of the strongest recognised indicators of two-year-old form: its winner, Gay Gallanta, would be quoted the following month as favourite for the 1995 One Thousand Guineas. However, Myself ran second again in the Washington Singer Stakes. Again, as at Ayr, the winner was a novice horse, the 3–1 second favourite, Lammtarra.

Myself's defeat was seen, at the time, as rather a fluke. She was not herself, said some of the reports; she had swerved to the right in the final furlong in a way that had cost her the race. Alex Scott, who trained Lammtarra, saw the result differently. His feeling was not that Myself had lost but that his horse had won. Taking the post-race quote of 33–1, he struck a thousand pound bet on Lammtarra to win the 1995 Derby.

The weekend after Ezzoud ran fourth behind the French horse, Carnegie, in the Prix de l'Arc de Triomphe, a seven-furlong two-year-old race called the Hyperion Conditions Stakes was run at Ascot. It was won, on not especially fast ground, in a time which broke a record that had stood for ten years. Celtic Swing had quickened so fiercely inside the last two furlongs that he finally finished eight lengths clear of the fancied Singspiel. After the Ayr run, his owner, Peter Savill, had backed him for the Derby at 250–1; now his price hovered around 14–1.

It is the Group One Dewhurst Stakes, however, which has come to form the most reliably acknowledged test of a two-year-old's worth. Run over seven furlongs at Newmarket, in the past thirty years it has been won by more subsequent Derby winners than any comparable race: Nijinsky, Mill Reef, Grundy, The Minstrel, Generous and Dr Devious. The 1994 field, assembled on 14 October, was strong. The race was won by the French-trained Pennekamp, who, after a tricky run, produced a smooth and decisive burst of speed in the final furlong. Quoted at 8–1 for the Two

Thousand Guineas, he revealed perhaps a little too much pace for a mile-and-a-half horse; his price for the Derby was therefore around 16–1.

This was how things stood in the middle of October. The senior handicapper with the British Horseracing Board, Geoffrey Gibbs, opined that the 1994 two-year-olds were of a high quality; ranked chief amongst them was a horse called Sri Pekan, winner of the Richmond Stakes at Goodwood and the Laurent-Perrier Stakes at Doncaster, and quoted as 7–1 favourite for the Two Thousand Guineas. Other highly ranked names were those of Munwar, winner of the Haynes, Hanson and Clark Stakes at Newbury, a race previously won by Shergar; Eltish, who won the Royal Lodge Stakes at Ascot and ran second in a USA Breeders' Cup race; and Chilly Billy. Lammtarra, who had injured himself slightly after the Newbury race and not run since, did not feature.

Among the fillies, which were regarded as especially good, the prominent names were those of Gay Gallanta, Myself and Harayir, third behind Gay Gallanta in the prestigious Cheveley Park Stakes. The betting on these horses for the 1995 classics shifted constantly and nervously, like a patient in a doctor's waiting-room. Each inward movement seemed to say two things at the same time: yes, that the bookmakers were protecting themselves, perhaps with far more caution than the horse merited; but also, that the shortening price was responding to some quickening in the horse, sudden and decisive as a movement in the market, a small signal perhaps of greatness to come.

In the middle of October, the markets were edging delicately around the two-year-olds, tightening here, loosening there; wondering, speculating, opining, hoping. It was all good fun, and it was all perfectly normal.

The Racing Post Trophy at Doncaster has only been run since 1961. A Group One mile race for two-year-olds, it lacks the prestige of the Dewhurst. In 1993 it was won by King's Theatre, but only Reference Point has gone on from it to win the Derby, though Linden Tree did run an honourable Derby second to Mill Reef.

On 22 October, however, it was won by Celtic Swing in a manner that clearly told his audience he could win not just the Derby, not just the Triple Crown, but the whole damn lot – anything you threw at him, from the carefully arranged pattern of Group races, he would catch and claim as his own. He won the Racing Post Trophy in such a way that the watching crowd felt they had never, even in their most glorified memories, seen such a horse before. As he galloped to the post, twelve lengths clear of Annus Mirabilis in second, with the field strung out behind him over almost seventy lengths, he seemed to take us back to the early days, when horses like Eclipse were able to move in a different world from those around them: 'Celtic Swing first – the rest nowhere.'

It wasn't just the distance by which he won, nor the fact that at a speed of forty-three miles an hour he seemed to be merely cantering. It was the ease of his huge stride, the knowing glint in his strong eye, the casual lift of his near-black neck, that compelled so absolutely. It seemed as though he did not need time to turn him into a myth. He was a myth already: the earthly Pegasus for which flat racing continually seeks. There were those who affected not to be impressed by him but even they, it somehow seemed, were using cynicism to protect themselves against the possible destruction of the myth.

What was extraordinary was that, if Celtic Swing were indeed all that people wanted him to be, he would destroy any notion of flat racing as a competition. There would have been no courageous battles to the winning post, jockey fighting against jockey, head bobbing against head. There would have been no breathtaking, final furlong swoops, as a horse suddenly surges from the pack and takes the race from the leaders on the line. There would have been no surprises, no reversals, no sport.

There would simply have been greatness; and the response to

Celtic Swing shows how deep the desire for this runs. For what stirred his spectators was the thought that he was not just a horse who won, or who won by a long way, but who won in a way that horses *didn't* win. This was not just Nijinsky or Mill Reef, whose greatness remained in the realm of their competitors. This was a horse that could win not just by yards, but by lengths, furlongs; something not just beyond the human and the known, but beyond dreams. This was a horse that could stretch our dreams further and further into the land of myth, and still make them come true.

Whether people acknowledged it or not, this was what they wanted from Celtic Swing. In their deepest hearts, they wanted to watch him run through the Guineas, the Derby, the St Leger, the King George and the Arc of 1995 as if he were racing on his own. They wanted what cannot be found in any other sport: absolute greatness. And they wanted the quest for it to be over.

Beyond this, what entranced people about Celtic Swing was his unlikeliness. For the past ten years or more, the provenance of the great horses could be predicted almost completely. They would be the offspring of Nijinsky, or Sadler's Wells, or Danzig; they would probably have been bred in the USA; and it was increasingly likely that they would be owned by an Arab, either Prince Fahd Salman, Prince Khalid Abdulla or, most likely of all, one of the four brothers of the Al Maktoum family, rulers of Dubai.

Celtic Swing, however, was a son of Damister, a stallion whose stud fee for 1994 had been £3,000 (Lammtarra's, when he retired at the end of 1995, was ten times that). Damister had run third in the 1985 Derby, thirteen lengths behind the victorious Slip Anchor. Whereas the progeny of Sadler's Wells won £767,795 in winning prize money in 1994, that of Damister earned £187,806, of which Celtic Swing accounted for more than £100,000. In fact, this figure made Damister a good deal more successful than most stallions, but he was twelve years old and established, by 1994, as a horse that could throw plenty that was decent and nothing that was great.

He had been mated to a well-bred mare called Celtic Ring by Lavinia, Duchess of Norfolk, whose daughter, Lady Herries, trained for Peter Savill. Savill was an extremely rich man, like most owners of flat racehorses. But he did not, like the Al Maktoum family, own large amounts of bloodstock from which to breed, and he had forty-nine horses in training in 1994, compared with the Al Maktoums' six hundred or so. He bought Celtic Swing for £20,000 on the advice of his jockey, Kevin Darley, who had ridden alongside the horse on Lady Herries' gallops and pronounced him the best two-year-old he had ever seen. Savill bought another horse from the Duchess of Norfolk at the same time. Opaline won at Sandown as a two-year-old and died, from colic, in the summer of 1994.

A latent xenophobia did raise itself in the racing public, at the prospect of an English-bred horse, running in an Englishman's colours (those of West Ham football club, no less, though imitating them was probably not Savill's intention), routing the vast organisation of the Al Maktoums. But there was something beyond that, something connected with the magic of Celtic Swing. It was the idea that a horse of this kind could flower in such unexpected soil: that the production of a great horse is not pre-ordained.

This was a liberating thought, somehow, in a world that can seem to grow ever tighter and more rarefied, circumscribed by the commercial mechanisms of stud farms, strangled by those etiolated lines of pedigree. It was, too, a relaxing thought. That a horse like Celtic Swing could have been raised in an English garden, by a woman who was perhaps as surprised by him as anyone else was, seemed to restore to the sport some of its simplicity and delight.

And of course it brought the horse closer to his public, in a way to which he seemed to respond. For all his supremacy, there was a paradoxical air of accessibility about him. His eye was bold, and an unusually arrogant crescent of white gleamed in its corner, but it also held a look of understanding: as if he knew what the public thought of him. Most fine flat racers carry a look which says that they know how good they are, but they tend, also, to keep this look to themselves, indifferently apart from those who watch them. Celtic Swing seemed to share it. He seemed to comport himself amongst people as if allowing them to worship him: assured, nerveless, nobly at ease.

On 22 October, he revealed something about the nature of flat racing which, a whole season later, has not been forgotten. The quotes of 5–2 for the Derby, and the handicap rating of 130 – the highest ever given to a two-year-old, and six pounds clear of Pennekamp's – were merely the signifiers of what had happened to the racing world. Its deepest desires had been opened within it, allowed to breathe without shame, by this big young horse and his simple victories. As with Ezzoud, I shall always be grateful to him.

What Celtic Swing did in the Racing Post Trophy would create a hunger in his public that, in 1995, he would be expected to fill. He would be greeted with an expectation not high, but absolute. We would wait, with unimaginable complacency, for him to act out fantasies of which we had already dreamed. If he failed, our disappointment too would be absolute; our hunger raging and unassuaged.

Flat racing decrees that the two-year-old horse is merely the presage of what is to come, and that only at three – and sometimes later than that – does a horse earn the right to be called great. There is good sense in that decree. The two-year-old races are constructed as brief indicators. The three-year-old contests are the real thing. The classics follow testing, bending courses; then, later in the season, races such as the Coral-Eclipse Stakes, the King George VI and Queen Elizabeth Diamond Stakes and the Prix de l'Arc de Triomphe are run against older, more powerful, more experienced horses.

And yet – even as a two-year-old – Celtic Swing did something very remarkable when, by the nature of his eruption into the racing world, he reminded it of the nature of its dreams. Maybe, if you chose to look at it a little differently, what he did on 22 October was enough.

34

III

BY COMPARISON, LAMMTARRA'S entrance into the racing season was a quiet one. It had charisma, but of a very different and self-contained type. His first victory was, in fact, indicative of what was to come: it was fantastically impressive, but was too unpredictable to be appreciated as such. As always, the horse was a beat ahead of his audience.

Comparisons with Celtic Swing reveal a double twist, which plays upon the idea of expectation confounded and confirmed. Lammtarra was the perfect horse in a way that Celtic Swing was not; Celtic Swing was the perfect horse in a way that Lammtarra was not. That is to say: Lammtarra had all the advantages of breeding, conformation and background. Celtic Swing had all the attributes of the wonder horse. And Lammtarra triumphed, finally, where Celtic Swing did not: in the arena of the 1995 racing season.

As thoroughbreds go, Lammtarra was a thoroughbred to end all thoroughbreds. He was a son of a Derby winner and an Oaks winner. His sire, Nijinsky, was one of the greatest horses of the century, his grandsire, Northern Dancer, one of the greatest stallions. His dam, Snow Bride, was the daughter of Blushing Groom, winner of the French Two Thousand Guineas, and of Awaasif, who won the Yorkshire Oaks and was placed in the Arc de Triomphe.

Lammtarra's Pedigree

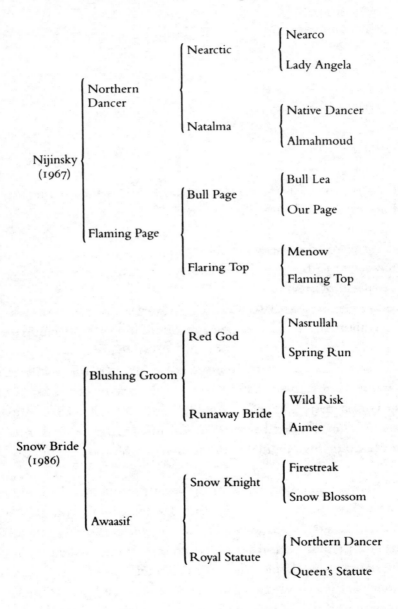

Awaasif was the daughter of Snow Knight, who won the 1974 Derby.

The impeccability of this breeding showed itself clearly in Lammtarra's conformation. He was not showy, in the way of Celtic Swing, with his high near-black neck and rolling eye; but when he emerged for his first appearance at Newbury he seemed to be possessed of a perfection that was so inevitable that he need draw no attention to it. He simply owned it. With his low-held head he seemed almost to deny it, in the way of the truly beautiful young. He had about him a rangy, rather callow look, accentuated by the short flaxen fringe that fell, like a schoolboy's, across his brow. A thin white tear streaked down his face, between his remote eyes; the lines of thick muscle were dark upon his chestnut coat, like the shadowy rub of velvet.

As well as breeding and beauty, Lammtarra enjoyed the incomparable advantage of being owned by the Al Maktoum family. He ran in the colours of Saeed bin Maktoum Al Maktoum, the nineteen-year-old son of Maktoum Al Maktoum, who as the eldest of the four brothers is the official ruler of Dubai.

The Al Maktoums have now been involved in flat racing for twenty years. It was in 1976 that a member of the family bought his first yearling. Sheikh Mohammed Al Maktoum, then aged twenty-eight, bought a filly for 6,200 guineas which, nine months later, won at Goodwood; by 1980 his interest in the sport had grown sixfold, and by 1985 he was its leading owner. Now all the Al Maktoum brothers own horses. Sheikh Hamdan, who owned the 1994 Derby winner Erhaab, has almost as many in training as Sheikh Mohammed, though Sheikh Maktoum (who owned Ezzoud), has far fewer, and the youngest brother, Sheikh Ahmed, only a handful. But it is Sheikh Mohammed whose name is most closely identified with flat racing. When Lammtarra won the Derby, most people seemed to think that the horse belonged to him.

Trained in the British Army and the RAF (he is now Dubai's minister of defence, as well as its Crown Prince), Sheikh Mohammed had been introduced to flat racing by his English lawyer. It was natural enough that an urbane Anglophile, such as he is, would gravitate towards the sport. But Sheikh Mohammed is also an Arabian horseman whose father, the late Sheikh Rashid, was a Bedouin warrior. Dealing with the thoroughbred, whose ancestors were ridden and bred by his own ancestors, seems to have filled a noble and primitive longing within him; and by the mid-1980s a social interest in racing had developed into a fascinated compulsion.

It was at this time that his influence, and that of his family, began to make itself most powerfully felt. At the USA sales, they were paying sums for yearlings that were beyond belief and beyond sense, inducing a feeling that, with their seemingly infinite wealth, the Al Maktoums were inflating the market to a point where no one but themselves could play in it. In fact, though, the market had already been inflated by the man who was, in the late 1970s and early 1980s, the most powerful force in racing: Robert Sangster.

Heir to the Vernons Pools fortune and a man who saw the sport as a genuinely commercial enterprise, he had formed a syndicate whose strategy for money-making was foolproof, so long as no one came along to challenge it. The plan was simple: Sangster bought yearlings with a view to their career as stallions. If they did enough on the track to be marketable at stud, then the Sangster syndicate was in profit. The only necessity was that Sangster should buy *any* yearling that *might* make a stallion, in order to have control over all the desirable bloodstock.

Sangster was guided in his purchases by the Irish trainer, Vincent O'Brien, whose incomparable instinct led him to advise that the syndicate should buy the progeny of Northern Dancer (had the situation arisen, Sangster would certainly have been prepared to spend a million or two on Lammtarra). By this strategy, the syndicate established the pre-eminence of a great stallion, whose offspring have dominated racing for the last thirty years; it also came to have control of horses such as The Minstrel, Golden Fleece, El Gran Senor and Storm Bird. And, in the inflated market that the syndicate itself had created, the stud value of these horses reached absurd and fantastic heights. In 1981 Storm Bird, who won a brilliant Dewhurst Stakes but ran only once as a three-year-old, was sold to an American stud owner as a stallion for $28 million. His purchaser had never even seen him.

It was in that same year that the Sangster domination of the market was first challenged by the Al Maktoum family. At the Keeneland Sales in Kentucky, Sheikh Mohammed and Robert Sangster bid against each other for two sons of Northern Dancer; the ferocity of their desire not to yield led to them spending a total sum of $6.8 million. Each bought one of the yearlings, both for a record price. The Sangster syndicate purchase, named Ballydoyle after O'Brien's stables in Tipperary, won nothing. The Al Maktoum yearling, Shareef Dancer, won the 1983 Irish Derby.

This was just luck; but, at the 1983 sales, it became clear that the Al Maktoum family was in a position to take control. It did not need, as Sangster did, to treat racing as a commercial enterprise. It could simply buy. That year at Keeneland, a Northern Dancer yearling came up for auction that the Sangster syndicate desperately *wanted* to own – they, after all, had uncovered the true worth of this stallion – but that the Al Maktoums *knew* they could own. This horse became the symbol of the struggle for dominance within the world of flat racing; bid struck against bid, as the yearling stalked delicately around the arena. Finally, and inevitably, Sheikh Mohammed triumphed with an offer of $10.2 million. The fact that the horse, Snaafi Dancer, could not run a yard made no difference. His purchase had signified, as clearly as was possible, the true power of the Al Maktoum family.

Perhaps out of bravado, Sangster did in fact pay a record price of

$13.1 million for another Northern Dancer yearling but, after this, a truce was reached that bidding of this kind would no longer take place. For Sheikh Mohammed, though, it would no longer be necessary. Sangster, whose years of supremacy had left him with a fine stock of thoroughbred blood, retreated from buying into breeding. In the falling market of the USA yearling sales, which bankrupted many over-borrowed American breeders, the Al Maktoums could simply buy and buy: vast, unprecedented numbers of horses.

They bought success at the same time, though not, perhaps, what their outlay deserved. Sheikh Mohammed has been champion flat owner in every year since 1985, except for 1990 when Sheikh Hamdan took the title from him. Nevertheless, in 1992, when Sheikh Mohammed had around 750 horses in training, costing around £1 billion to buy and £350,000 a week to keep, he did not win a single Group One race for the first six months of the season. Now, however, with the greater knowledge and greater reserves of bloodstock that the Al Maktoum family has acquired, they, like Robert Sangster, are in a position to breed rather than buy.

The family owns a large number of stud farms, mostly in England but also in Ireland and the USA. It was at the American farm of Sheikh Maktoum's Gainsborough Stud that Lammtarra was born, in 1992. He was the second foal of Snow Bride, and one of Nijinsky's last; aged twenty-five, the great horse died at Claiborne Farm, Kentucky, where he had lived since 1971, in the year that perhaps his finest son was born.

Lammtarra arrived in Newmarket, at the Oak House Stables of Alex Scott, in the winter of 1993. Scott was one of several trainers employed by the Al Maktoum family. Their number included the flamboyant Henry Cecil, champion trainer for the tenth time in 1993; Michael Stoute, champion in 1994 and trainer of Ezzoud; John Dunlop, trainer of Erhaab; Major Dick Hern, who trained the filly Harayir for Sheikh Hamdan; André Fabre, who trained Pennekamp in France for Sheikh Mohammed, and was considered by many the best in Europe; and John Gosden, who trained another promising two-year-old called Tamure, and whose Sheikh Mohammed-owned horses were all ridden by Frankie Dettori.

Scott, at thirty-three, was far less established than any of these, but was regarded as having the potential to equal them. The son of a Steward at Ascot and Kempton Park, he had first been attached to a stable when riding point-to-points in Yorkshire. After this he had worked as an assistant, first with Tom Jones in Newmarket, where Michael Stoute started his career, then with Major Hern in Berkshire. This was where Scott came to the attention of the Al Maktoum family. Rigorous men as they are, they appreciated the perfectionism of his attitude.

In 1989, at the request of Sheikh Maktoum, Scott took over Oak House Stables, and inherited a full yard of fifty-six horses with excellent staff to look after them. This was luck of the kind that changes a trainer's life. So rarefied and exalted is the world of their trade, that simply climbing to reach it can take all of their energy; it is far easier to start near the top. It may be true that you earn your own luck, but you have, first, to be lucky enough to be in a position to earn it. Henry Cecil, for example, who was without doubt the most celebrated trainer of the last twenty years, bounced confidently off an initial double deal of good fortune. He inherited a fine Newmarket yard called Freemason Lodge from his stepfather, Sir Cecil Boyd-Rochfort, and took over Warren Place, perhaps the very best yard in Newmarket, on the retirement of his ex-father-in-law, Sir Noel Murless.

There is, too, a class thing here. The position from which both Cecil and Scott earned their luck was placed high within the social hierarchy; in racing, this still counts for something. Indeed, Cecil's luck began to desert him when he left his wife, Julie, for a girl who worked in his yard: affairs are commonplace in the enclosed

Newmarket community, but divorcing a much-respected woman for a sexy young thing is regarded as a poor show. Of course there are successful trainers, like ex–footballer Mick Channon, whose provenance is less obviously patrician. Yet many owners – including, it would seem, the Al Maktoums – still like to hear the velvet in their trainers' voices, and to be greeted by the impeccable tilt of their James Lock hat in the paddock. They like to feel, perhaps, that their thoroughbreds are living amongst people with an implicit understanding of the mysteries of the aristocracy.

For Alex Scott, the essential combination of luck and ability brought success very quickly. Within three seasons, he had trained two sprinters who were champions of their year. In 1989, Cadeaux Genereux – now a promising sire – won the Group One July Cup at Newmarket and the Nunthorpe Stakes at York. In 1991, Sheikh Albadou won the Breeders' Cup Sprint in the USA.

The Breeders' Cup comprises seven races, run on a single afternoon at the end of the European racing year. Their vast prize money totals $10 million. They were conceived, in 1984, on the American scale: to attract the best horses in the world, and perhaps to displace the Prix de l'Arc de Triomphe as the climax of the season. It was always impossible that this should happen. The differences between European and American racing are simply too great, as is shown by the fact that American horses rarely try to prove themselves here.

Five of the seven Breeders' Cup races are run on dirt, a surface to which European horses are unaccustomed. American horses run on drugs that are banned in Europe; and American jockeying is a comparatively tough, unsubtle business which, in pursuit of victory, will ride horses flat out from the first furlong. By 1995, the English had won three of the seventy-seven Breeders' Cup races that had been run. There is more luck than usual involved with these races, and entering a horse in them is a speculative rather than calculable decision. Nevertheless, the fact that Sheikh Albadou was one of the three to have triumphed in that harsh, unknown arena is a tribute to both the horse and his trainer.

Because of his two champions, Alex Scott was regarded as a trainer of good sprint horses; but he had also won the Irish and Italian Oaks with Possessive Dancer, and Sheikh Maktoum's horse Fraam won the 1994 Golden Mile at Goodwood. This horse also, incidentally, ran at Newbury on the day of Lammtarra's first race.

In 1986, Scott married Julia Mackenzie, with whom he had three children. Three years later, at the end of his successful first season at Oak House, he suffered a depression that was possibly brought on by stress and over-work. He spent three nights in a nursing home, and was given medication which he continued to take periodically.

In 1992, he moved with his family to Glebe House, a beautiful Queen Anne house in Cheveley. The attached stud farm was run, in all but name, by an Irishman called William 'Clem' O'Brien, who had worked there as a groom since 1975. Head lad at Oak House Stables, charged with the task of running the yard, was former stable jockey David Phipps. A likeable and articulate man in his late thirties, Phipps worked for Alex Scott's predecessor, the late Olivier Douieb, and now works for Scott's successor, Ed Dunlop.

Alex Scott had wanted Lammtarra from the first moment he saw him, as a yearling in the USA, in July 1993. 'He was struck by him immediately,' says Julia Scott. 'He just liked him. So he asked if he could train him – you didn't necessarily get what you asked for, but you might as well have a go. And he got him.' Of course Lammtarra was beautifully bred and formed, a big and rangy yearling with plenty of growth in him; anyone with an eye for a horse could have seen as much; but Alex Scott saw something more. It was as if he had intuited, from this horse, that the time might have come to move into a different sphere: the sphere of greatness.

This is a feeling that cannot be explained, and that therefore may sound absurd, but the best trainers all have it, and know how to trust it. Something in a horse speaks to something in them. This happened several times throughout the magnificent career of Vincent O'Brien, perhaps the most intuitive of them all. In 1968, for example, he went to Canada to buy a yearling son of Ribot (dual winner of the Arc) for the American owner, Charles Engelhard. He returned to Ireland with Nijinsky instead. 'He appealed to me,' he said, of the greatest horse he ever trained: the mysteries of the thoroughbred remained intact.

But when Lammtarra came to Newmarket he was, of course, a yearling like any other. 'There were about ten colts altogether,' says David Phipps, 'and they all arrived about ten o'clock at night, all came off the box together. And basically you don't take much notice of 'em. They're the yearlings. You know, as long as they're all right after the journey, that's about it really. And then the next morning, you start looking at 'em, start breaking 'em in.

'He looked a nice horse, Lammtarra, he looked a real nice horse. He looked like he had scope, he'd grow and be a nice horse. But, I mean, nobody knew at that time that he'd win the Derby, King George, Arc.

'When we started to work him, after Christmas, he worked well but not outstanding. Nice. Once they start to canter, you can look at them and, the way they move, the way they handle themselves, you can say – he's a nice horse. And some'll be like big fat slobs – if they were human they'd be couch potatoes. They're all different.

'But, you know, you've got nothing in the yard to work him with to find out how good he is, at that time. They're all coming along together, the two-year-olds. But you've got a couple of older horses, that you use as lead horses, and usually they're nice two-year-olds if they can work well with the older horses. And he did.

'Temperamentally he was good to break in, you didn't know he was in the yard. He was a gentleman in the box. And then he went out on the Heath' (the training gallops at Newmarket) 'and we did things with him which he accepted. But when he started to really work, after Christmas, and we used to take him through the town to go up the canter, after he'd done it a couple of days he didn't want to do it. He didn't want to go from the Newmarket side of the road, where we were, to the Bury side. He got there and stopped. He got something in his mind, and he just wouldn't do it. He thought, I'll take on this morning. But eventually we said to him, look, you've got to do this – chased him up a bit – and away he went.'

It was when Lammtarra, as a very young two-year-old, began to gallop rather than merely canter, that Alex Scott received what he sensed to be confirmation of his promise. Julia Scott: 'He did say, I think this could be a Derby winner. But then that's the art of a trainer – to be able to know class when you see it. Alex hadn't had many good mile-and-a-half horses – we did have a horse that was one of the favourites for the French Derby, and we got rather hyped up about him, but he wasn't that good. But it was amazing really – he did always talk about Lammtarra as a Derby horse. It was almost as though he was psychic about it. He was always very, very excited about him.'

A strange picture emerges here of this young horse, doing on the one hand all the normal, routine things that any horse in training would do; and on the other hand being thought of, dreamed of, as a winner of racing's most glittering prize. It is a picture that became all the clearer when I visited Oak House: now, like Sheikh Maktoum's stud, called Gainsborough. The vast, modern stables, with their tall roofs and spare corridors, emanate the almost banal purposefulness of a factory. The glamour of the horses, standing behind their painted doors, is quietened. Their individuality here is not that of fame, but of character: the good one, the one that plays you up. The only thing that marks them out is a little white tab outside each box, a printed slip that bears their name and breeding.

And yet the sense of possibility pervades those corridors like the potent hush of a cloister. Their stillness is full of imminence: you know what stands behind each of those stable doors. Because of this there is a peculiar, restrained thrill about the little white tabs, such inadequate symbols of what they might represent. I imagine Lammtarra's, when he arrived as a nameless yearling: Ch 1992 Nijinsky – Snow Bride by Blushing Groom. The box where he stood is empty when I visit, but it is easy to imagine him standing behind its door. There is a sense of Alex Scott's presence too. Some of the little white tabs bear the name of Cadeaux Genereux, Scott's first champion, whose progeny now stand in their father's yard.

Opinions differ as to whether Lammtarra was expected, by his connections, to win his first race, the Washington Singer Stakes at Newbury. 'We said, if we're second, we've run well,' says David Phipps. 'The filly Myself, she's a Group winner, she'd run at Royal Ascot and that, and we thought – we won't beat her.' Julia Scott, however, says that 'Alex knew Newbury would be a bit short for him, but he hoped that the class would tell and it did.'

Walter Swinburn, who rode Lammtarra in the race, had never been on his back before that day. 'All I knew was that he was a good-looking horse, he stood out physically. He was pretty damn near perfect. But I didn't know what to expect. I did know that he was a lazy horse at home, and that if he ran a good race it would wake him up. Because he wasn't getting any better; he would plant himself at times and not move. He was – as the Irish would say – taking the mickey. But in my experience the best horses do have a kink.'

Swinburn, then thirty-three, had come to prominence in 1981 when he rode Shergar to a ten-length victory in the Derby. Several classic wins followed, mostly for the Al Maktoum family: Unite in the 1987 Oaks; Doyoun in the 1988 Two Thousand Guineas; Musical Bliss, Hatoof and Sayyedati in the One Thousand Guineas of 1989, 1992 and 1993. He also won the notorious 1986 Derby, in which Greville Starkey mistimed so badly the run of Dancing Brave – winner of every other great race in the season – that he lost by half a length to Shahrastani. In early 1996, he sustained multiple injuries after a freak fall when riding in Hong Kong; at the time of writing it is hoped that he will recover fully and resume his career.

Swinburn is not a showy jockey, like Carson or Dettori. He has an air of deceptive delicacy when he rides, an almost ghostly look. But his timing is smooth and beautiful, and he has inexpressible class. Certainly he rode Lammtarra with a perfect instinct.

The race at Newbury was broadcast by the BBC, and it is fascinating to watch the recording, in which all the protagonists in this remarkable story wander around the sunlit, sparsely-peopled course with such relaxation. The result of the race before Lammtarra's took an age to judge – it was finally pronounced a dead-heat – and so its presentation ceremony is overlapped by the parade for the Washington Singer. Into the corner of the picture stroll Swinburn and Scott, talking intently. Then a low-hanging head crosses the frame, its subdued dark eye looking almost bruised against the warm coat, its bewilderment not quite concealed within self-containment.

The first couple of seconds in Lammtarra's racing career are in-auspicious: when the starting stalls opened, he simply didn't move. Of course, he had no way of knowing that this was what it was all about, getting out and getting going. So familiar are we with the spectacle of that mass leap forwards, we forget that, for a novice horse, everything about a race is new and extraordinary. When he did come out of the stalls, he ambled towards the back of the six-strong field with his whole body wearing that earlier look of sup-pressed confusion. Wigberto, ridden by Frankie Dettori, was the clear leader. Myself was well-placed in third, and looked as though she could win the race at any time she chose.

After about half a mile, Lammtarra was still ambling along the inside rail. Swinburn, who had allowed this in the early stages, now began to ask the horse for a little more, but got nothing; for another furlong, nothing. Myself took the lead and seemed about to run

47

away from the field. Still nothing. 'I don't like to use the whip on young horses, but I had to, because' – Swinburn says, in a tone of faint self-mockery – 'it looked at one stage as if it was going to be embarrassing.' And suddenly, then, he got something. Suddenly, with a furlong left to run, there were three horses clear of the rest: Myself, Petoskin and Lammtarra.

Somewhere within the final furlong is a moment of quickening, a surge from Lammtarra that has about it the look of greatness. It is so easy, so decisive, so absolute. But so young and green is the horse that produces this moment that he scarcely knows what to do with it; like a drunk inside a Ferrari, he veers left from the rail to the centre of the course, forcing Swinburn to change the whip to his left hand in order to straighten him out. At the same time, perhaps from fatigue, Myself also swerves, cutting across Petoskin to meet Lammtarra in the middle. For a moment she seems to check the power of his surge. Then he finds it again. He passes the line three-quarters of a length clear of the Group winner filly. At the very instant of doing so, his ears prick up: as if he has suddenly realised the point of what he had been doing.

And then, of course, he wanted to go on doing it. 'I'll never forget,' says Swinburn, 'after the race I just couldn't pull him up.' The energy that had been stirred, so briefly, in his body rippled through his legs as he was manoeuvred, still trying to run, into the winners' enclosure. His head reared, frothing like a Delacroix. His quarters reversed dangerously into the brittle, suited PR girls who teetered around his stamping hooves. He had been shown, for the first time, the true power that he possessed, then after a few seconds had been asked to harness it again; and the effort of restraint was lacing his back with sweat. Angry whiteness foamed from his mouth, around his neck, beneath his tail. He looked almost ugly; his coat dank, his eye wild and sullen. Perhaps he never looked more magnificent. It was all there, then, waiting for him to unleash his power and take it. Alex Scott, glancing at Lammtarra across the enclosure with a look of proud, casual possessiveness, seems from his expression to sense as much. He backed him that very afternoon for the Derby.

I watched the recording of that race after I had seen the triumphs of 1995. I watched it over and over, trying to realise that this raw baby colt was the great Lammtarra. In so doing, I learned more about flat racing than in ten or more years of trotting between paddock and Tote and grandstand at Royal Ascot.

I learned that the flat racehorse, for much or even – if it retires young – all of its career, is like a child: endlessly susceptible to new experience. I learned that, as with a child, you can watch the process of the horse's own learning: like when Lammtarra suddenly jolted out of the stalls, two seconds after they opened; or when he straightened up for Swinburn, and began to try and win; or when he passed the post and lifted his ears to the new sensation of victory.

Above all, I learned what gives this sport its dangerous, gut thrill: the partnership between horse and jockey. At its best, when it is in perfect balance, there is no greater partnership in sport. Of course, it can easily be sent out of balance. A horse can be completely unresponsive; a jockey can pull a race, make a horse look slower than it really is, in order to cheat the handicapper; or a particularly skilled jockey can, occasionally, win a race with a horse who was not really good enough to win.

This is something that many followers of the sport will admire. They cite certain victories of Lester Piggott, which they say no other jockey could have achieved and which form, in a sense, the finest possible testimony to Piggott's genius. If they mean by this that he elicited something from a horse which no other jockey could find – as he did in the 1972 Derby, pushing the lazy but talented Roberto to the line by an inch or so – then that is, perhaps, the supreme example of the horse-jockey partnership. If, however, they mean that Piggott beat better horses by better jockeyship, then

49

that, ultimately, is uninteresting to me. If a horse isn't good enough to win, then I feel that it *shouldn't* win. Winning a race by luck, or by another's mistake, as when Shahrastani won the Derby in 1986, is a different matter – that is the kind of thing that can always happen in sport – but winning by superior strategy, admirable though it may be, sends the horse and jockey partnership out of balance. It makes the jockey more important then the horse, and that is not what flat racing is about.

The true partnership is the one between a living force incomparable with any other in sport, and the courage and instinct required to control it. What fascinates me most about it is that the jockey has, as far as is possible, to become the horse. He has to see the race in the way that the horse does. To hear him talk about a run is to realise this: the pronouns 'I', 'he', 'she', 'we' are all tangled up together, as if it is impossible to know whether jockey or horse was the one that got cut off, or went for the gap, or won, or lost.

But the jockey also has to see beyond what the horse sees. He has to see what the horse wants to do and find a way to do it; to see what it fears and find a way to avoid it. Up to a point a jockey has to be guided by a horse, but he in his turn has to guide it. Theirs is, at its best, a partnership of unusual beauty, in which two become one. But it has been earned by the fact that both the will of the horse and the will of the jockey have been stretched to the limit. It breathes, and it sweats, and it is real, and precarious.

At the time of the Washington Singer Stakes, Lammtarra would have weighed something over one thousand pounds; Swinburn weighed not much more than one hundred. Just to look at the hoof-tracks left at the end of the race, and the wayward diagonal that they describe, shows the course that Lammtarra ran and that Swinburn had to control. To see the fierce little movements of Swinburn's arms, like those of a wounded bird trying to take flight, shows the urgent force that was needed to make Lammtarra race. And all on no food! Of course, after Ezzoud, probably any ride is easy, and Swinburn says that 'the only work I had to do was in the beginning of the race.' The rest – the straightening and finishing – would be instinctive to a man of Swinburn's experience and ability. But I learned from watching it an absolute respect for the partnership between horse and jockey; and a respect for the jockey almost as great as that for the horse.

After the Newbury race, says David Phipps, 'every time Lammtarra worked, he worked better and better. And we thought: we've got a good horse here.

'But he was lazy, even then. You had to keep him up to it. The thing was, when you galloped him at home you'd put him behind, then you'd pull him out; he'd join the other horses, put his head in front, then he'd think: I've done enough. And the thing is, horses like that, they'll never win more than a length or so, but they'll keep going. They'll just keep pulling a little bit out. They'll just do enough, all the time.

'You see them – they pull it out at the last minute and just hit the line at the right time. A jockey knows. If he hits the front too soon the horse will stop. He's not stopping because he wants to stop. He's stopping because he thinks: I've done it. And that was what Lammtarra was like.'

No fool, in other words. But he continued to improve, and was being prepared for a campaign of autumn races, when he sustained a slight twist to a joint which finished his two-year-old career. It was around this time that Sheikh Mohammed let it be known that he wanted Lammtarra to spend the winter not in Newmarket, but in Dubai.

The idea of wintering horses in the sun was not a new one. Sir Ivor, who won the 1968 Derby, was partly prepared for the race in Italy. If an owner could afford it, it was clearly a very sensible thing to do. Athletes like Linford Christie train throughout the winter in countries like Australia, where their muscles can relax and develop, so that they can begin the season in an advanced condition of fitness. A racehorse could theoretically benefit in the same way.

Newmarket outside the racing season is a place of almost primeval bleakness: the thick, white sky over the Heath seems to reach to the ground. Wintering a horse in such surroundings, or indeed anywhere within Northern Europe, is a difficult business, because preparations are always vulnerable to the vagaries of climate. It was therefore natural, and perhaps inevitable, that the Al Maktoums should think of taking horses away to the sun: this was, after all, their own home.

The first intimation that the 'Dubai experiment' might have far-reaching consequences came at the beginning of the 1994 season, when a filly named Balanchine wintered in the desert. A daughter of the $28 million stallion Storm Bird, she had been bought by the Al Maktoums from Robert Sangster. When she returned to England, she ran second in the One Thousand Guineas. The distance was a little too short for her, but she lost the race by inches.

Over the course of the season, the intimation turned into proof. Balanchine went on to win the Oaks and the Irish Derby, and to become the top-rated three-year-old of 1994. Other horses that had wintered in Dubai – such as Cezanne, who won the Irish Champion Stakes – also achieved considerable success. Whether it was the winter campaign that had helped these horses, or whether they were sufficiently superior to have won these victories anyway, was in a sense an academic point. The real point was that the Al Maktoum family would *perceive* the Dubai experiment to have worked.

Certainly, wintering in the sun might give a horse an advantage at the start of the season. A two-year-old turning three is a baby, still growing and developing, and the warmth of the desert would be a kindly place for it to do so: in the three months that Balanchine spent in Dubai, the temperature was a constant 75°F, broken by a single half hour of rain. Perhaps, even, some atavistic memory would have caused her hooves to embrace the feel of sand beneath them; the low flat gallop of the thoroughbred is said to come from its desert origins.

There is no doubt that Balanchine looked glorious in the One Thousand Guineas. Her dark chestnut coat was sun-glossed amid the other still-roughened backs, her muscles stood alert, and she ran as if she was never more ready to do so. But by the time of the Oaks, in June, it is surely likely that any advantage would have been eroded; by the time of the Irish Derby, it would undoubtedly have been. A horse cannot sustain an unnatural peak. If wintering in Dubai had given her an undeserved early supremacy, then Balanchine would not have improved throughout the season as she did (nor, indeed, would Cezanne, whose greatest triumph came in the autumn). The fact is that Balanchine would have been a magnificent filly if she had spent the winter in Reykjavik. And this, of course, was something that Sheikh Mohammed had already guessed when he took her home with him in October 1993. This was why he wanted her to have what he perceived to be the best.

The first year that wintering in Dubai had been tried was not, in fact, 1993. A few horses had gone to the desert the previous year, one of which, Dayflower, ran fifth in the 1993 One Thousand Guineas; but it was in 1993 that the experiment became an experiment no longer. Fifty horses went to Dubai, twenty-four of which contested the 1994 English flat race season, in the colours of a company named Godolphin Racing. Eleven of these horses, including Balanchine, were stabled with a Dubai trainer named Hilal Ibrahim. Few people were in any doubt that both Godolphin Racing and Hilal Ibrahim meant one thing: Sheikh Mohammed.

In fact, Godolphin is a company owned by both Sheikh Mohammed and his elder brother, Sheikh Maktoum. His family is always keen to maintain the Dubai ruler's interest in racing; even to the point of giving him several of their best horses, including

Lammtarra's dam, Snow Bride. Nevertheless, there is little doubt that the true, passional inspiration behind Godolphin is Sheikh Mohammed's love of racing and, above all, of the horse, a love that led him to take this step nearer to its heart. Throughout the winter he could have his favourite horses in his own care, under his own supervision, in the place that his family ruled. It is no wonder that the victories of Balanchine brought him such especial joy; after the Irish Derby his saturnine, hawkish face was smiling like a child's as he returned the embraces of Frankie Dettori, tremulously shaking his jockey's hand in the air, like a referee giving a fight to a new champion.

By 1994, the Godolphin operation had grown to the point where more than seventy horses were sent to winter at the Al Quoz stables in Dubai. Around half of these would be sold to race in the desert, thus bolstering the growth of the sport and increasing the attraction of Dubai as a tourist destination. Of those that returned to Europe, the best – in the opinion of Sheikh Mohammed – would again be stabled with an Arab trainer, Saeed bin Suroor, who had been established at the Moulton Paddocks yard in Newmarket.

Though an ex-policeman, Suroor really was a trainer. He had sold his car to finance his stables in Dubai, which he had set up within two converted garages. He was, nonetheless, a front man. He admitted as much when, asked what the plans were for this or that Godolphin horse, he replied: 'I will ask Sheikh Mohammed. We are a team. Sheikh Mohammed will decide later.' Despite the fact that Godolphin was, indeed, a team – whose principals comprised Suroor, the Godolphin racing manager Simon Crisford, and John Gosden's former assistant Jeremy Noseda – Sheikh Mohammed was the real trainer of these horses. They were his personal élite, the ones that he had selected, and studied, and grown to know. Through his wealth, he owned horses in numbers that gave him a stake in the whole of flat racing, and made him an invaluable part of its world. But, with Godolphin, he was concerned solely and intimately with the pursuit of greatness.

The most damaging charge that can be made against Godolphin is that it uses European trainers. It allows them to do the hard, fraught and delicate work of turning a racehorse from a yearling to a two-year-old; then takes the horse away from them. It deprives these trainers of the fees that they would earn and that they have, to an extent, already earned. It deprives them, too, of the money and glory that the Godolphin horses are capable of bringing them. Sheikh Mohammed, as has already been made clear, only takes the best.

In 1994, the two-year-olds that were taken to Dubai included Lammtarra and Tamayaz, both with Alex Scott; and Vettori, Moonshell and Classic Cliché, who had shown great promise with Henry Cecil. Balanchine went back to the desert, and two other fine three-year-olds were also taken: Moonax, trained by Barry Hills, who had won the English and French St Legers, and Halling, who had won the Cambridgeshire handicap with John Gosden.

It was not a rule of Godolphin that these horses would be trained, on their return, by Saeed bin Suroor. The original trainer might get them back. But the departures for Dubai inevitably created a great deal of uncertainty. Trainers, however successful, were infected with the fear that any decent horse in their yard would be bought by the Al Maktoums – if they didn't own it already – and removed, either for three months or forever.

Working for the family is probably an anxious business anyway. A group of people with such power and wealth also has, by definition, the right to be as exacting as it thinks fit. With the institution of Godolphin, this anxiety would be increased to an alarming intensity: the smallest slip, the least hint of ignorance or vulnerability on the part of a trainer, would become horribly magnified in his mind. How much, he would think, would it count against him, when the calculations were made as to which horses should go to Dubai?

It has been said that some trainers do, to an extent, deserve to have these feelings of instability inflicted upon them. Like the USA breeders in the 1980s, who milked Robert Sangster and the Arabs for millions of dollars (even, it is said, sometimes putting fake bidders into the ring to inflate the yearling prices), in the earlier days the Al Maktoum trainers made a great deal of money out of their owners. Training fees in the more fashionable yards, like Henry Cecil's, were upwards of £25,000 a year per horse; and, if one drove a hard bargain, there were remarkably lucrative shares in stallions to be negotiated.

During a time of recession, when English money was relatively scarce, the Al Maktoums had kept Newmarket buoyant. They protected flat racing: maintaining its position of aloof security whilst, around it, other sports fought desperately for sponsorship and survival. Racing owes a great deal to their unquestioning support. Could they really be blamed for starting to question that support a little, for doing things on their own terms? After years in which their wealth had conferred such patronage, was it surprising that it was now asserting its autonomy?

There is no doubt that some trainers had had it too good for too long. However, the argument that they were now being given their come-uppance was rather thin. It was torn by a single fact: that Halling was not returned to John Gosden at the start of the 1995 season. In this there was no slight intended to Gosden, who remained one of Sheikh Mohammed's most favoured trainers. It was simply that Halling was seen as one of the best; and Sheikh Mohammed wanted the horse for himself.

Logic says that Sheikh Mohammed is absolutely within his rights. Nevertheless, the emotions resist the idea of Godolphin. It seems to bend the rules of the way things are done to an alarming degree: to take part of the racing season away from us. A horse that benefits from the triumphs and prestige of this season should also, we somehow feel, suffer its privations. The idea that money can buy the privilege of a winter in the sun seems wrong: a feeling that is the most illogical of all, since what money can buy is what flat racing is all about.

There is, too, a sense that Godolphin has finally made competition against the Al Maktoums an impossible thing. For some years now, races have frequently been dominated by the colours of the brothers, but the fact that they were all in opposition to each other meant that this was no different, really, from having a race full of horses owned by Robert Sangster, Lord Weinstock, Lord Howard de Walden and the Aga Khan. However, if those four had all got together and formed a horse-owning company, that would have felt rather different. It would have felt like Godolphin Racing.

Does it matter, though? I couldn't care less who owns the horses, so long as I can see them run to the best of their ability. To the average spectator, the competition within races is not between owners, and it is purest sentiment to imagine that the Al Maktoums are in some way preventing the 'ordinary' owner from competing in the sport. At the highest level, the ordinary owner has *never* been able to compete.

The other charge against Godolphin, that horses are being taken from trainers who have already done the hardest work of all, matters far more. The only consolation is that this must remain a limited enterprise, or else its power would surely be diminished; also, the number of horses owned by the Al Maktoums is still so large that no decent trainer would be deprived by it of a living. Finally, though, there is very little that trainers can do about Godolphin. The Al Maktoums own the horses, and they can do with them whatever they wish. That, it would seem, is unanswerable.

It might also be intolerable, were it not for the fact that the respect that the family has towards the sport, and the horse, is palpable. If they have become its guardians, they are responsible and dignified ones. Their assertion of autonomy has been, indeed, a far less damaging one than it could have been. They continue to provide hugely in money and work, and also in other areas such as veterinary research, the sponsorship of races and the provision of the all-weather Al Bahathri Gallop at Newmarket. Their sense of the sport's history can be seen in the names that they give to their enterprises: Sheikh Mohammed's Darley Stud, after the Darley Arabian; Sheikh Maktoum's Gainsborough Stud, after the 1918 Derby winner, whose pink and white colours still tile the stud's big stallion box; and Godolphin Racing itself, after the Godolphin Arabian.

They retain their respect for European, especially English, racing; and above all for the horse. For this alone, respect is due back to them. How can one doubt a man who, like Sheikh Mohammed, says of the thoroughbred: 'I love this breed. These animals are not machines; they are soul and flesh and blood'? His understanding of his horses is profound; his desire to deepen it is infinite. Godolphin is not, for him, a money-making strategy, or a revenge upon greedy trainers, or a means to destroy competition. To think as much is absurd. For Sheikh Mohammed, the journey that takes the thoroughbred back to Arabia is, quite simply, the road to greatness.

For Alex Scott, however, the fact remained that it was taking from him his best horse. Indeed, it was taking from him his best two horses: for Tamayaz was regarded as a prospect only slightly less promising than Lammtarra. As Julia Scott says: 'Alex wasn't very happy about Lammtarra going to Dubai, but he was assured he was going to get him back. I think that reassured him a bit, but he really didn't want him out of his care. He was concerned. It had been done before, but it was quite a new thing and we hadn't had any horses go out there before.

'It's hard to say whether it's the winter over there that's benefiting them, or what they're doing, or have done, over here. Their coats do look incredible when they come back, so it probably does do them good – you can tell them a mile off, when they've been there. But in fact both Lammtarra and Tamayaz had a problem in Dubai.'

David Phipps, however, who believed strongly in the help that wintering in the desert could give to a horse, interpreted the situation a little differently: 'We were over the moon that he was going to Dubai, and we were over the moon that he was coming back.'

'It was the end of September, the Maktoums came, and they looked round with Alex. And they said to him, Lammtarra will come back to the yard. Another horse will be sent out there – that was Tamayaz – but you'll get 'em both back. And that night Alex came and said to me: Great, we've got 'em back. And off he went. And that's the last time I ever saw him.'

Alex Scott was murdered about an hour after this meeting, on 30 September 1994. At around 5.15 pm, he stood within the imminent stillness of Oak House and heard, behind one of the doors in those cloistered corridors, the sound of his future as it shifted quietly on its hooves. He held, then, the promise of glory, like an infinitely precious and fragile ornament. At 6.10 pm, in the barn at his Glebe Stud home, it was shattered by a single gunshot wound to the chest.

The next morning, police found William 'Clem' O'Brien, the 57-year-old groom at Glebe Stud, sitting among the horses in the stable block. He was still holding the shotgun with which he had murdered Scott.

There had been difficulties between the two men from the time that the Scotts took over the stud. O'Brien had become accustomed to running the farm according to his own rules and opinions; Tony Shead, who had owned Glebe Stud, had been frequently absent. He had considered O'Brien to be a useful and unusually hard worker, and when he sold the stud he told the Scotts that they should keep the groom on. Julia Scott was later to call this 'the biggest mistake of our lives'.

O'Brien became increasingly resentful of the fact that his

unquestioned authority had been usurped. He argued with every order that Alex Scott gave to him, and complained of what he had previously relished: being under-staffed and over-worked. He was particularly unhappy about dealing with Julia Scott, despite the fact that she had extensive knowledge of horses; like her husband she had been a point-to-point rider, and indeed she now runs Glebe House Stud. O'Brien seems to have believed, as some Irishmen do, that his nationality gave him privileged access to the world of the racing animal. Certainly, it is true that the Irish tend to have an instinct with horses, and it was also true that O'Brien knew how to run a stud, but those with a real understanding would never need to bully. It was reported that O'Brien would use a pitchfork on those who disobeyed him, both stable lads and horses.

Not long before the murder, the difficulties between O'Brien and Scott reached crisis point. During an argument about a lost sale, O'Brien made reference to his employer's earlier depressions, saying that he should have 'stayed in the loony bin'. This was not the first time he had expressed this opinion: for some while he had been telling people that 'your man there is mad'. By then, Scott had had enough. He sent a letter confirming O'Brien's resignation, and asked him to return a signed copy, which he did not do. Instead he told several people that he was 'finished', and that he was going to 'get' Alex Scott.

On the evening of 30 September, Scott went with his gardener, Christopher Forster, to visit O'Brien in his bungalow on the Glebe Stud land, and ask for his keys. Julia Scott said afterwards that she was uneasy about this. 'I thought that O'Brien might punch him or something.'

She was drying her hair, in her bedroom, when Forster ran to the house and told her that her husband had been shot. O'Brien had invited Scott into the barn and, as Scott turned away from him, shot him in the back at point blank range, saying: 'This is for you, you bastard.' Forster prevented Julia Scott from going to her husband, fearful for her because O'Brien was still in the grounds. She waited twenty minutes for the police to arrive. Only then, when the paramedics went to Alex Scott, did she learn that he was dead.

It is very hard to imagine this horror happening within the stately, spacious grounds of Glebe House. It is a calm place. Despite the presence of three children, there is an emptiness about it, yet it is quietly resonant with the restrained, matter-of-fact dignity of Julia Scott. As at Oak House, the presence of Alex Scott is very strong; but here it is made manifest. Everywhere, there are photographs of him, with his family and with his victorious horses. In the hall hangs the most familiar and triumphant of all tributes to his memory: the chestnut horse in the green and white colours, becoming speed incarnate in the final furlong at Epsom.

At his trial, William O'Brien claimed that he 'just flipped'. He said: 'I just grabbed the gun and that was it. Everything I worked for had gone. It had all just fallen at my feet.' He had denied murder, but admitted manslaughter on the grounds of provocation, saying that Scott had treated him like 'a slave'. However, this plea was dismissed. The judge who sentenced him to life imprisonment told him that he had, 'for reasons it is difficult to fathom, totally lost your temper and, in a moment of passion, picked up a gun and shot Mr Scott.'

Yet it is not, perhaps, so difficult to understand why O'Brien shot his employer. In a perverse kind of way, there were similarities between the two men. Both were almost obsessively hard workers, both were exhaustive perfectionists, both demanded the highest of standards from those who worked for them. Both were, in essence, doing the same job. This may have made the differences between them all the more intolerable to O'Brien.

Alex Scott had, after all, what amounted to a perfect life. Born into privilege, the son of a Lord-Lieutenant of Hampshire, educated at Eton and Cambridge, he had acquired a wife who understood his passions and dreams, three children and a beautiful home. He had had the luck to take over Oak House Stables and the ability to succeed there. He enjoyed the patronage of racing's most influential owners. He had horses of great promise in his yard. He moved easily within the enclosed world of Newmarket, and the wider world of his sport. He had wealth, charisma, position and youth, and a future ready to deliver everything that such a past might expect.

Beyond the spectacle of Scott's perfection was, too, the reality of what it meant in O'Brien's life. There is, after all, a powerful hierarchy within the racing world. Dedication to the horse unites those who work within the sport, but it is impossible to ignore the almost feudal sense of a dependency of servant upon master. Beneath the protected, moneyed sphere of racing's élite – the glamorous owner and the gentleman trainer, standing together in a sunlit paddock – seethes a sweating, reeking, grafting proletariat of work riders and apprentices, stud workers and stable hands. The fact that the people at the top may work just as hard as those at the bottom is not the point. They sound different; they look different; and, within the world of racing, they *are* different.

The photographs that accompany reports of William O'Brien's trial make this all too clear. There, grouped upon a sofa, sits the handsome Scott family: Alex and Julia with their refined smiles and upright backs, their eldest son kneeling between them, their daughter on her father's knee and the baby boy held by his mother. There, across the page, is the face of William O'Brien: bespectacled, unfriendly, with a look of coarse, rustic evil. It is not hard to see that for this man to have been in the power of the other one, obliged to bow to his commands and live in the shadow of his home, might have been unbearable. The desire to destroy, to reverse the order of their lives, might have become overwhelming for O'Brien.

There is no way of knowing if that is what helped to motivate the murder of Alex Scott. Certainly O'Brien was eager to seize upon the one apparent flaw in his employer's perfect life: the mental depressions that he suffered (something that again, perhaps, brought him perversely close to O'Brien). And, certainly, the desire to destroy perfection – to dim its golden glow, to crack its seemingly impenetrable veneer, to take away its future – is a natural one to those whose lives are murky with envy. It is there in every burglary that despoils a proudly-maintained house, in every attack upon a pretty young girl, in every act of vandalism.

It has been there before, too, in the racing world. In 1983, when Shergar was taken from his stable by the IRA, the obvious motive was money: believing the horse to belong to the Aga Khan, the terrorists held him to ransom, then murdered him when they learned that he was, in fact, owned by a syndicate which was unlikely to meet their demands. But the crime could only have been committed by those whose shabby, pathetic lives were as far away as possible from the perfection that the horse symbolised. After all, those who cannot feel the pleasure in greatness will, inevitably, seek to kill that pleasure for those who can.

Alex Scott's friend, Lord Howland, spoke the address at his memorial service, on 18 October: 'To say he was one of the great trainers is something time has cruelly robbed us of, but he was well down the road to being a great trainer.' Many trainers and jockeys were at the church, including Walter Swinburn, who had been Scott's friend as well as his rider. 'All we can do now,' he said, after the service, 'is hope that Lammtarra will win the Derby for us.'

IV

In the spring, Celtic Swing looked down from the height of his proud, near-black neck upon the flat racing season. It lay before him, stretching from March to November. Within it were the great races that his public was waiting for him to win. He was never so powerful as when he stood, as at the top of a hill, upon the brink of fulfilling the dreams that he had created.

About a month elapsed between the start of the season proper, with the Lincoln Handicap at Doncaster, and Celtic Swing's first race of the year at Newbury. During that time he became, in so far as is possible for a flat racehorse, a personality. His trainer, Lady Herries, was advised by a PR company that, in order to diffuse the endless questioning about Celtic Swing, the thing to do would be to invite the racing press to take tea with him.

Lady Herries being what she is – a lady – the party was perfectly judged. It was a mixture of good hospitality and good taste, thrown by someone who was happy to share her sense of good fortune. There were game pasties and sloe gin; there were the surroundings of the Angmering estate in West Sussex, with its fourteen thousand acres and its two mile grass gallop; there was the lady herself and her husband, former Test cricketer, Sir Colin Cowdrey; and finally, there was the horse, shimmering out of his box on to the lawn in front of his trainer's house, weaving nervelessly among his worshippers, an invisible laurel wreath around his taut, black ears.

Photographs and press reports of the party were extensive. However hard they tried to conceal it, they conveyed an almost childlike sense of goodwill – a party atmosphere of their own, indeed – towards Celtic Swing and the people who wanted to share him with us. This was something different, presenting the horse to his public in this way ('Can you imagine Henry Cecil doing it?' was apparently the most frequently-spoken remark at the party). It may have been a PR exercise, but it was also something simpler and more generous. It was as though both Lady Herries and Celtic Swing's owner, Peter Savill, realising the deep pleasure that their horse had brought, wanted to increase that pleasure, both for themselves and the public, by sharing their own surprise and delight. They wanted to feel what is not necessarily felt in flat racing: the love and warmth of the crowd.

So breathtakingly ephemeral are the victories in this sport, they acquire a full weight of anticipation and celebration only if they have already been imagined. In the minds of the crowd, the race must have been run before: its emotions of expectation, hope, fear and fulfilment must have been felt. Never was this more true than it was with Celtic Swing. He had been placed in those stalls a thousand times already; over and over again he had ambled through the furlongs, his dark body poised for movement; he had increased his stride and pulled away from the rest more times than could be counted. We could see it. We knew how he would look when he strode, huge head tossing and nodding, to his rightful place in the winners' enclosure. We knew how we would feel then.

It would not be quite the same feeling as when Red Rum won his third Grand National, or Desert Orchid his fourth King George VI Chase; or even when Brown Jack, perhaps the most popular flat racehorse of the century, won at the age of ten his sixth Queen Alexandra Stakes, at Ascot in 1934. There was weeping at those victories. Hearts cracked with joy, leaked sentiment into hardened bodies that had seen it all before. Those victories were like Christmas ought to be: bright parcels full of the very best memories which, when opened, confronted people again with their younger, happier, more innocent selves.

Celtic Swing's would not be quite such a victory. It would be a Shakespearean, not a Dickensian ending, because flat racing is not a sport for sentiment: it disdains it, demanding instead emotions of a more rigorous kind. To see Celtic Swing win would be an experience painful not in its nostalgia, but in its splendour. It would be a victory that did not merely stretch and fill our hearts, as Red Rum's had done, but stretched and filled our dreams. Look, it would say, this is what the world can create: this animal that can power, like a god, away from his own kind. How much more then is he powering away from us! Celtic Swing would be no people's champion, however much we might wish it. How could anyone think as much, when they saw his proud stallion separateness, and heard the terrible thunder in his hooves? What had such a creature to do with our human clamour, the wave of betting slips and the feverish cheers? Like all the others before him, Eclipse and St Simon and Nijinsky, he would run alone towards greatness, and we would know it. But we would know, too, that we had come as close as we could to running along with him. The dreams that he had created now belonged to us, and their fulfilment would be ours as well as his.

The waiting for it to happen was unbearable. I cut out the horse's photograph and stuck it in my kitchen, looking at it every day as Celtic Swing's first race drew nearer. The knowing arrogance in it took my breath away every time I saw it: how could a horse's neck arch so high, a body be so big and certain, an eye roll with such command? Life seemed to be a magnificent business, full of power and delight and mystery, when I looked into that glancing stare. Sometimes I would wish that it was not necessary for the horse to come down from the top of the Angmering gallops, in order to fulfil our dreams for us. Let him stand there forever, a part of me thought. The dreams are there anyway. He has done what he has done.

Meanwhile, the horse who was to win the races that, at that time, belonged to Celtic Swing, was in an equine hospital in Dubai. Lammtarra was dying. He was, it seemed, destined for a life as tragically unfulfilled as that of his trainer. All that perfection was to be wasted. Those in Dubai expected him to die; those in England had forgotten that he had ever lived. When racing journalists went out to see the Godolphin horses in Dubai, a month or so before they took tea with Celtic Swing, they did not see Lammtarra. His name was not mentioned.

If he had been thought of in the spring of 1995, it would have been, perhaps, in this way: as a horse who had had one decent run, seven months earlier, and whose life had been sent off course by the death of the man who believed in his potential. And now he too was dying? Ah, terrible. He might have been rather good, like Alex Scott. A waste. An unlucky horse. But then there are plenty of those.

The only thing was that there are not plenty of horses like Lammtarra. He was a thoroughbred amongst thoroughbreds – a true aristocrat, with an aristocrat's obduracy – and he was not a horse to lie down meekly and die. Something that might have killed a gentler animal was not, he was damn sure, going to kill him. Anyone who has seen him run would know that it would take a lot to kill such a horse. It is very hard, in fact, to imagine him almost dead in the spring of 1995: not just because of what he was subsequently to achieve, nor because he has an air of vibrant vitality – he does not. It is because of his self-containment. There is nothing pitiable about him, nothing that seems to ask for care of the kind that he then needed. If he had died, there would have been no pathos there at all, no big uncomprehending eyes staring helplessly into those of his vets. It would have been a death to make you angry rather than sad: it would have seemed, like Alex Scott's, so *wrong*. For Lammtarra's nature was that of a survivor. He was, above all, a fighter. He had a will whose depth could not be fathomed and which loved, always, to take things to the edge before conquering them. And he had some important running to do yet; he had not yet vindicated his trainer's judgement. He was not going to be finished by bad luck.

There had been an abscess in his lung which had failed, repeatedly, to respond to antibiotics. Despite constant tests, it had been very hard to discover exactly how to treat him. Eventually, though, after fourteen days in the equine hospital, he began to rally. Superior veterinary skills, which Sheikh Mohammed had promoted both in Europe and Dubai, were the visible agents of his recovery; but the horse himself was hell-bent upon living. The year before, Balanchine had also been saved by Sheikh Mohammed's vets when she was close to death with colic; but she, too, was a tough horse. However, she never ran again as she had done in 1994, when she took on the colts in the Irish Derby and showed them what was what. It is one thing for a horse to survive and race; it is another for it to survive and triumph.

By late March it was clear that Lammtarra was, at least, going to survive and run again. Walter Swinburn saw him at that time: 'I had heard about his illness and – well, it didn't sound too great. When I saw him, he was just about walking. He looked awful. But he had pulled through, and that's the character of the horse.' Those who worked with Godolphin imagined that Lammtarra would return to England and, when fully fit, contest some of the races that came later in the season. Sheikh Mohammed, however, thought differently. There was no question in his mind but that the stumbling, barely-breathing horse should be prepared for the Derby. The race was then about ten weeks away, three hundred and two days after the single outing at Newbury.

It was as if Sheikh Mohammed had come to see Lammtarra

through the eyes of Alex Scott: as if he had assumed Scott's role as the horse's guide, as the believer in his potential greatness. Sheikh Mohammed had, from the first, valued the presence of Lammtarra in Dubai. The fact that his elder brother, Sheikh Maktoum, had entrusted his son Saeed's horse to Godolphin showed his approval of the operation, especially as the horse has shown such promise. But Sheikh Mohammed had also seen Lammtarra close to death; had seen his own equine hospital fight for the horse's life; had seen above all the horse fight for himself. Now he wanted everything for Lammtarra. The horse had been born with so much, and had nearly lost it all; but now he had his life back, and the patronage of the most influential man in racing, and he was about to recoup on his advantages.

The invisible preparation began. Lammtarra learned again to do what he had done before; he trotted, then cantered, then galloped around an oval track, constructed in Dubai, with the tight, left-handed turns of Epsom. In England, meanwhile, Celtic Swing galloped a powerful straight mile for the assembled press on the all-weather at Angmering. It was reported that he looked as good as ever, his stride as huge and devouring as it had been in the Racing Post Trophy; and that he was to run his first race of 1995 at Newbury, in the seven furlong Greenham Stakes, on 22 April.

The year before, Turtle Island had won the Greenham by eight lengths. This was the least that his public expected from Celtic Swing. There was no doubt, whatsoever, that he would win the race, but that would not be enough. He had to win it like Celtic Swing. There was an almost hysterical jollity in the atmosphere of the race meeting, a communal frenzied smile. It was like the prelude to a wedding in which every guest knows the groom to be a wonderful loving chap, but not what he got up to the night before at his stag party.

To see Celtic Swing in the paddock was an extraordinary thing.

After all that had been written and said and thought, it was a shock to realise that he took a real, corporeal form. He emerged into the arena rhythmically, slowly, with a relaxation that created a calm space amid all that amassed expectancy. It seemed impossible that he should not feel the atmosphere; it seemed impossible that he would simply run, like any other horse; it seemed impossible that our dreams should at last have to meet reality. It all seemed impossible. This horse had lived too long in fantasies and imaginings. When I saw him in the paddock, I felt that it would be impossible for the reality to compete.

And yet he looked like the dream horse: that thick neck, that size, that gleam, that dark head crossed, in its familiar way, with white trickling blaze and white noseband. He looked like Celtic Swing. He was the same horse that had run into another world in the Racing Post Trophy. But I couldn't rid myself of the strange, illogical notion that he was no longer free to run into that world: that, somehow, our world was now too much with him, and that the races had been won in our heads before they had, in fact, been run.

Two furlongs out in the Greenham Stakes, it seemed quite clear that Celtic Swing was going to win this race, at least, in reality. He had only to quicken in the way that he did, and the painful accumulation of waiting would dissolve. Please God, let it happen, else what would I do with it all, this mass of feeling inside me? He had only to quicken in the way that he did. That was it. That was what everyone knew. When the commentator, on the recording of the race, says to that poised white noseband: 'And this is the moment', his own voice is tremulous with the knowledge that those five, bare words carry the weight of six months of expectation. This was the moment. And he did quicken: his giant stride took him instantly away from the rest of the field. And for another moment it seemed as though the dreams were about to come true, that he was going to leave the other horses in their other, more ordinary world while he ran back into his own: 'Celtic Swing first – the rest nowhere.'

It did not quite happen. Bahri, ridden by Willie Carson, went with him. He could not get very near to him and, despite Kevin Darley's urgings, Celtic Swing seemed to be going easily, almost lazily, his body upright in contrast to Bahri's low outstretching. He seemed, too, to be gazing with interest into the crowd. He had quickened when it mattered but he did not do so again. Still, he won the race comfortably, by a length and a quarter.

I remember going out to dinner that night with my father, where inevitably we discussed the Greenham Stakes. Unspoken, like a yearning hum beneath our conversation, was what we wanted to believe about the race. Out loud, we voiced our misgivings, as if by letting them buzz around us we would be able to swat them dead: 'Well, perhaps he hasn't really trained on?'. . . 'Carson said his horse could have won – perhaps he's right?'. . . 'Perhaps he's lazy?'. . . 'Perhaps he was only beating rubbish when he was a two-year-old?'. . . 'Perhaps – I don't know – perhaps he's not as good as everyone thought?'. . . And only then would we remember that Celtic Swing had in fact won the race, easily, disdainfully, a length and a quarter away from a horse at the edge of his limit, and nine lengths clear of the third.

I still thought that he would win the Two Thousand Guineas, and then the Derby. I remembered *Timeform*, in which it had been written that, although there was no such thing as a racing certainty, the closest thing possible to it was that Celtic Swing would win those two races. I thought about them, nonetheless, with a kind of fear, because the subtle and illogical disappointments of the Greenham Stakes had placed Celtic Swing upon a fine line. On one side of it was fulfilment; on the other side was nothing; and I could not bear the thought of him stepping on to that side. He was quoted at odds-on for the Guineas, a fact in which I took comfort. I just wanted it over, and won.

★

The build-up to the Two Thousand Guineas, which was run on 6 May, was like a house of cards made of hot bricks. Every day, in the newspapers, there was the story about how Pennekamp was to run, how Bahri was to take on Celtic Swing again, how Sri Pekan was withdrawn with a pulled muscle. There were reports of how Celtic Swing galloped on the all-weather and was sharper than before, as if his race had given him an edge; of how Pennekamp had won the Prix Djebel in France over six furlongs, but had not particularly impressed; of how, on a subsequent gallop, he had pulled away from his companions in a way that had excited his French trainer, André Fabre.

There were interviews with Celtic Swing's owner, Peter Savill, which gave readers the sound of fighting talk when spoken by a gentleman: 'My horse has been winning so easily that he hasn't yet been in a true race. I'm sure he will be in one at Newmarket, and I've no doubt he will buckle down when the time comes. I'd be very confident if it was what I call an average Two Thousand Guineas, but this is clearly above average . . . Something's got to give.'

There was the opinion of Willie Carson, one of the shrewdest of racing judges, who was to ride Bahri again in the Guineas: 'They are all getting carried away by Celtic Swing. For me, he didn't put up a very good trial . . . I can see him getting beaten in the Guineas. I am not saying he will be beaten, but it would not surprise me at all.'

There were fears, whose quiet expression was almost smothered by the sound of the pre-race hype, that the ground might be a little too hard for Celtic Swing's powerful, pummelling stride. He had run his best race at Doncaster in late October, when his hooves were able to gather up the turf as they travelled it. There was also a reference, quickly forgotten, to his slightly crooked front legs, and the fact that they needed beneath them a little forgiving softness.

There was an extraordinary feature in *The Times* called the Race of Legends. In this, the form of the best post-war Guineas winners was analysed with that of Celtic Swing, to discover what the result of a race between them would have been. For the purposes of the exercise, the race was run on good going. Its line-up included Nijinsky; Sir Ivor; El Gran Senor; Brigadier Gerard, the last horse to beat Mill Reef; Dancing Brave, who won everything except the Derby in 1986; Zafonic, whom André Fabre described as the best two-year-old he ever trained; and Tudor Minstrel who, under Gordon Richards, won the 1947 Guineas by eight lengths.

The Times provided a 'commentary' upon the Race of Legends by Peter O'Sullevan. It even quoted odds, supplied by Ladbrokes, which had Tudor Minstrel as 7-2 favourite, and Celtic Swing at 14–1. They were proved to be accurate when it was judged, by analysis of the Two Thousand Guineas form only, that the race would have been won by Tudor Minstrel, with Brigadier Gerard second and El Gran Senor third. Nijinsky was fourth. It was considered that Zafonic would have come closer had the ground been fast. It was also thought that Celtic Swing would have run third, rather than seventh, had the ground been a little softer. This opinion, which had been expressed here within an enchanting piece of make-believe, began to acquire the force of reality as the sun continued to shine upon Newmarket.

But Celtic Swing was still odds-on for the Two Thousand Guineas. Sheikh Mohammed's Pennekamp, his closest rival in the market, could be backed at 5–1. Tudor Minstrel had not been odds-on, nor had Brigadier Gerard, nor El Gran Senor, nor Dancing Brave; nor any of them except Zafonic and Nijinsky, with their startling two-year-old form. Absolute certainty might have gone from the minds of Celtic Swing's public, but his victory was still seen as almost inevitable. The party was still going on: it only required the rush of air, as Celtic Swing flew away from the field, to make the balloons and bunting flutter with joy.

★

Again, it seemed not quite believable when Celtic Swing emerged into the paddock before the Two Thousand Guineas. The faint doubts about the Greenham Stakes, the front legs, the ground, did not disappear at the sight of him. But they rose and settled, like sunlit dust, invisible except for a sudden, shimmering flash in the corner of the eye.

He looked superb as ever in the paddock; different, I thought, from the others. Of course, I thought this partly because I expected him to look different. But that was, partly, the point. He looked as if he knew that this was expected of him, and he arched his neck to it as he trod his calm circles before the worshipping spectators. He looked nothing like Pennekamp, for example, who was almost drab in his professional self-containment. André Fabre and Sheikh Mohammed watched him beadily, severely: like the dark czars of racing, they stood ranged, across the paddock, against the smiling, openly tense gentility of Peter Savill and his amiable lady trainer.

Bahri was there, too, and Chilly Billy, horses that Celtic Swing had beaten; Green Perfume, whom Pennekamp had beaten in the Dewhurst; and Painter's Row, who had won the Craven Stakes earlier in the season. But only Pennekamp was being spoken of as a worthy rival, and even then an unlikely one. Only a single odds-on shot had lost the Two Thousand Guineas this century. Geoffrey Gibbs, the senior handicapper, said that, on the form, Celtic Swing should win the race by three or four lengths.

Two furlongs out, he quickened as ever, breaking joyfully into his big, easy, open stride. I felt, then, that he was going to win; but I also felt that winning the Two Thousand Guineas could not be that simple. On the outside, head pushing like a snake's, was Pennekamp. Pull away, pull away, I thought, moving my own head forwards for Celtic Swing. I heard the flat, falling note in my voice – 'He's not going to do it' – and at the same time a question: if I let the words out into the air, might not events be able to destroy them? Then I felt my heart break a little as Pennekamp went past Celtic Swing, and turned flat racing into sport again.

But then he came back, fighting to the line. So conclusive, so cataclysmic was the moment in which Celtic Swing was overtaken for the first time, it was hard to realise that he lost the Two Thousand Guineas by only a head: it was, as the American magazine, *Sports Illustrated*, wrote of Nijinsky's defeat in the 1970 Prix de l'Arc de Triomphe, 'one head that cost a crown'. The circumstances of that lost race were, of course, very different from those of the 1995 Guineas: Nijinsky was already a proven champion, though the weight of expectation upon him in the Arc was probably no greater than upon Celtic Swing. Essentially, the two defeats were the same, in that they both created the same sense that events had painfully, indifferently, betrayed us.

Perhaps the cruellest thing of all was that it *was* just a head, because the feeling persisted that Celtic Swing could, indeed should, have won the race. When he went to the front, two furlongs out, he took the lead and then, as at Newbury, refused to stretch it. It was obvious then that Pennekamp would overtake him. However, when Celtic Swing realised that this had happened – it took a few moments but it was, after all, something new to him – he began to race again. He made up a length or so on Pennekamp in the final hundred yards. André Fabre said that this was because Pennekamp also had a tendency to reach the front and simply stay there. What were we to make of that? Both horses had surged and both horses had idled; but Pennekamp had done it at the right time.

There was the other factor, of the hardened ground, which Pennekamp had liked and Celtic Swing had not. What did that mean? Did it mean that, if the ground had been softer, Celtic Swing would have won in his familiar style? Did it mean that he was still great, but not on fast ground? The ironic truth seemed to be that what had, indeed, made him potentially great – that huge, open stride, which subjected the yielding turf to its mastery – had also prevented his greatness being realised.

There was something else, something harder to explain. It was there in the look of him in the paddock, so different from the remote purposefulness of Pennekamp. It was there when he hit the front, in the simple way he had always done, and then relaxed. It was as if his mind had come off the job: as if, in some strange way, the belief that he had already won these races had been communicated to him. *That* was what had seemed wrong in the Greenham Stakes, that interested gaze into the crowd as Bahri came up behind him; not his running.

And meanwhile there was Pennekamp, whose own neck now seemed to arch and reveal its full beauty, though it did not gleam as Celtic Swing's had done. He had won the Two Thousand Guineas in near-record time, with third-placed Bahri two lengths behind him; further than he had been behind Celtic Swing in the Greenham. He was quick and decisive as a bullet, and every inch of him was packed with class. Perhaps Pennekamp was a great horse. Perhaps allegiance – which now hung limp and broken over the racing season, like a fractured wrist – should move instantly to the horse that could beat Celtic Swing.

The trouble was that I did not know him. On 6 May 1995, he was Ezzoud when he beat Erhaab in the Coral-Eclipse, he was Carnegie when he beat Ezzoud in the Arc: he was the one that had taken from me the imagined race and given me, instead, its reality. And, in this case, it was a huge and wrenching displacement. It was as if Pennekamp and his sport had decided that it was time to remind their public of two truths: that every race is different from every one that has been run before, and that every horse in it is capable of doing something that it has never yet done.

All sport has this capacity for ruthlessness. Because it is regulated, it gives us the illusion that, unlike life, it can be controlled; but within its regulations it remains defiantly life-like. This is especially true of flat racing. No sport is less susceptible to expectation, to prediction, to the converging will of the crowd. Flat racing is not easy on its public. It cares nothing for accumulations of hope, and dreams that yearn for fulfilment. It conducts itself according to its own, more stringent laws: the laws of the thoroughbred horse.

But faith in Celtic Swing was not yet extinguished. The weeks before the Epsom Derby were, as in the build-up to the Two Thousand Guineas, filled with speculation concerning the horse. This time, however, there was no joyous party atmosphere about it and it was of a less exalted, more confused kind: not whether Celtic Swing would win the Derby, but whether he would run.

His connections, who had seemed before the Guineas as ready as everyone else to see in Celtic Swing an absolute of perfection, were now, understandably, proffering mitigating factors for the horse's defeat. These factors – the familiar ones of hard ground and crooked legs – were also being debated as possible reasons for withdrawing Celtic Swing from the Derby field.

Popular opinion was, of course, that the horse should run. The Derby needed him and he needed the Derby. It would be unfair, unsporting, to separate them from each other. It was a perfectly reasonable opinion but I, for one, did not share it: I did not want the horse to run. I still cherished my dreams of him, and I feared their complete destruction. I felt that if he ran in another race – not the one that he had, in the minds of so many of us, already won – this could not quite happen. It was not a logical view; after all, the worst had in a sense already happened, and either the Derby would confirm it or, miraculously, show it to have been an unfortunate fluke. But I feared, obscurely, the horse's humiliation. He had not asked us to put him in the position that we did, standing on the brink of the season like a god. And so he should not, as he ran his own Derby with such youthful joy, be asked to bear the weight of our childish disappointment.

I much preferred the idea of Pennekamp running in the Derby. It had never been certain that he would stay a mile and a half, and his finishing speed in the Guineas would seem to have left the matter in doubt; though, as his trainer said, horses that win the Derby are not always bred to do so. Sir Ivor was an example of this. The fact that much of the race moves downhill enables them to get the mile and a half, and at the end they can simply burn off the true stayers with their superior pace.

Anyway I was selfishly comfortable with the idea of Pennekamp being tested. My feelings had nothing to lose and everything to gain. Either he would be beaten in the race, which could be attributed to lack of stamina; or else he would win, which would mean that Celtic Swing had lost to a great horse. Such are the calculations in the minds of those who follow, at a worshipping distance, the flat racing season.

Meanwhile, the preparations for the Derby continued around the drama that was being played out centre stage. Quietly, without fanfare, the other contenders emerged from the wings. Tamure, Sheikh Mohammed's second string Derby horse, won at Newbury on the day before the Greenham Stakes. As 1993 Derby winner Commander in Chief had done before him, he also won the Glasgow Stakes at York. The handsome colt Presenting – trained, like Tamure, by John Gosden – won at Newmarket on the day before the Two Thousand Guineas.

Munwar, owned by Sheikh Hamdan, won the Derby Trial at Lingfield. The Sheikh had two other entrants in the race: Daffaq, who had run a distant fourth to Lammtarra at Newbury, and was there solely to run as pacemaker for Munwar; and Fahal, who had finished almost forty lengths behind Celtic Swing at Doncaster, but was regarded as having an each-way chance in the Derby. Recently he had run third at Goodwood to a small, inexpensive (£54,000) horse named Pentire, who was not entered for the Derby, although he had won the prestigious Classic Trial at Sandown. In it he beat Singspiel, from whom Celtic Swing had finished eight lengths clear at Ascot, by a head.

Spectrum, trained by Peter Chapple-Hyam, won the Irish Two Thousand Guineas though, as with Pennekamp, there was doubt about his ability to stay a mile and a half. However, his jockey John Reid had said of him that: 'but for Celtic Swing, you would have hyped Spectrum all winter.' This impressed me so much that I backed the horse.

Lammtarra returned from Dubai around the time of the Two Thousand Guineas. He was stabled with Saeed bin Suroor, at Moulton Paddocks in Newmarket, and seemed to have made a full recovery. As Walter Swinburn says, implying subtly that his illness had not killed the little devil inside him: 'His manners at home hadn't changed, but it was nice to see that, after what he'd been through. He was just the same. He felt impressive, but he wouldn't necessarily show it.' He was one of two Godolphin horses entered in the Derby; the other, Vettori, won the French Two Thousand Guineas, but neither was accorded much attention in the press.

What was reported, continually, was the state of the ground at Epsom. There had been no rain on the course for a month, which was therefore watered throughout much of May, and said to be 'good, with good to firm patches' (bloody hard, in other words). There were some people who felt that the course should not be watered so heavily – that it was being done, in fact, to placate Peter Savill and persuade him to run his horse – but the truth is that it would almost certainly have been done anyway. It just would not have been news. This was news, though, every day: the press was not giving up on Celtic Swing yet.

Also news was the fact that Savill maintained an open telephone link to the weather centre, waiting to hear of rain; and that he had employed a prominent veterinarian to analyse the effect of fast ground upon Celtic Swing. This vet concluded that, in the last two furlongs of the Guineas, when the horse had been running down-hill on hard turf, his stride had shortened by around twelve inches.

This, of course, suggested something else beyond the fact that Celtic Swing disliked firm ground. It implied that travelling down-hill made the problem worse, and forced the crooked front legs to swing erratically as they tried to cope with it (this can actually be seen on a recording of the Guineas: from the knee down Celtic Swing's legs seem almost to be flying out sideways). Epsom's Derby course rises steeply for almost five furlongs, then turns a corner and moves abruptly downhill. It is perhaps the most difficult course in the country.

Peter Savill would, of course, have always known this. He knew it when Celtic Swing was a two-year-old with, presumably, the same front legs and huge stride. Had the horse won the Guineas, or even had there been less publicity about him, there is little doubt that he would have run in the Derby: hard ground, hill and all. Now, how-ever, it became quite obvious that, despite all the public prayers for rain and debates about the course, Celtic Swing was not going to run. It had been obvious, really, from the moment that Pennekamp went past him in the Two Thousand Guineas.

So it was hard to be surprised when it was announced, on 1 June, that Celtic Swing was to contest the Prix du Jockey-Club, or French Derby (a race that had been won in 1986 by Pen-nekamp's sire, Bering). This would be run at Chantilly, where there was rain and no hills, on the Sunday before its English equivalent. A supplement of 250,000 francs was paid to enter Celtic Swing at this late stage. Peter Savill did not say, even then, that his horse would not run at Epsom; technically, the possibility was still there and, perhaps, he wanted to believe that it *was* still possible.

He was criticised for running Celtic Swing in France and, almost certainly, avoiding Epsom and the rematch with Pennekamp. In fact, it was nobody else's business what he did. However, he did not say as much but instead insisted, politely, that he was doing what was best for his horse: it would be wrong, he said, to race such a horse on such a track if there was no give in the ground. Of course, it sounded as though he was making excuses. But it was true that he was doing the best for the horse. He was protecting him from those who had dreamed of his greatness and who wanted, through the absolute judgement of the Epsom Derby, to see those dreams either fulfilled or destroyed forever.

They wanted to *know* what to feel about Celtic Swing; now, they were in a state of yearning confusion. Should they still wait to worship him, or should they forget that they had ever wanted to do so? If he won at Epsom, he would be everything; if he lost, he could safely be thought of as nothing, and the quest for greatness could move on. At the moment, Celtic Swing was something, but nobody quite knew what.

His victory in the French Derby did not make it any clearer. This was partly because Chantilly was not the expected arena: the imagined drama in our minds was unprepared for this change of scene. It was partly, too, because although he won the race, he did not win it like Celtic Swing. He won on guts, not greatness. He won in the way that he might, perhaps, have won the Two Thousand Guineas: going to the front early, failing to pull away, being attacked, then fighting back to pass the line half a length clear. Perhaps he was only now learning what he had to do. In this instance, though, Poliglote in second did not overtake as Pennekamp had done; nor, it was said, did he have anything of Pennekamp's quality. In fact, he had won the Group One Criterium de St-Cloud as a two-year-old, and done so in a way that showed him to be a real fighter. In third was Sheikh Mohammed's Winged Love. He had finished well enough to be only a short head behind Poliglote.

It was all very different from what had been imagined, when Celtic Swing was 9–1 to win the Triple Crown, and when it seemed that the racing season would not need to deepen and unfold, in the way that it always did, because its events were already known to us. We had thought that the season would reach an early climax, which would simply continue to intensify: it would be like Celtic Swing when he won the Racing Post Trophy. Now, instead, its mysteries were still to be penetrated.

And somehow, Celtic Swing was no longer a part of them. The deepest mystery of all – that of his greatness – had been exposed, though not explained. The French Derby held something different from the usual victories of flat racehorses, which have little time for sentiment or for dreams; this brave, narrow win of Celtic Swing's touched more tender emotions. I cried as I watched it. When the horse passed the line, I whooped along with the English contingent at Chantilly; but, inside, I felt that what had been satisfied was not the voracious public hunger for his greatness, but something smaller and more private instead.

'Thank God' was the uppermost thought in my head: there was an almost overwhelming sense of relief that the worst had not happened, that something had been saved, that the accumulations of hope had been loosened a little. I felt, too, a strange pity. This horse still had the look of glory about him, his pride in himself was still supreme; he did not know that those whose expectations he had created, but not fulfilled, no longer saw him in that way.

Some of the press were hard on him the next day, much harder than they had been when he ran second. It made me angry. Celtic Swing's victory may not have been what was expected, but that did not mean that it had no value. But from some journalists there was no 'Thank God'. There was just 'So what?' I remember a particularly snide piece, which criticised the French Derby field – inaccurately, since Classic Cliché in fourth was highly regarded, and Winged Love in third had recently run stride for stride with Pennekamp on the gallops. It even criticised the race itself, branding it a mere imitator of our proper English Derby, and ignoring the fact that it was notoriously difficult for a horse to travel to France and win. It was a deliberate attempt to take all pleasure from what had happened, and to mock those who were determined to feel it.

Perhaps such members of the press felt that Celtic Swing had made them look silly. For all the talk now of crooked legs and indifferent two-year-old opposition (again, not quite true, as their runs against the Derby field were proving), it was the press who had called him the 'wonder horse', they who had taken such pleasure in their tea on the lawn with him. Perhaps, beneath that brisk desire to brush aside all memories and dreams, there was a real disappointment. It would have been better expressed than denied.

How ridiculous it all was, anyway! This was a horse who had won one classic and had almost won two, a horse that any of us would have been thrilled to own. If we had known less of him at the start of the 1995 season, we would, after the French Derby, have thought that Celtic Swing was pretty damn good – as, indeed, he was. He was a damn good racehorse.

If we had known less of him, what would his classic win have been? It might have been the start of a quest for greatness; but, because we knew too much, it was the end. We had, perhaps, seen it in the wrong way. We had made ourselves too important a part of the spectacle–spectator equation. We had willed events. We had expected the horse to be great rather than letting him surprise us; but, once the quest has begun, the desire to push it to its destination is irresistible. We had all wanted it from Celtic Swing, so much.

When we did not get it, a less noble desire emerged: to deny the pleasure that the quest itself had brought, even though it did not reach its expected end. This was what some of the press were doing, the day after the French Derby. Celtic Swing had been everything. Now – well, he wasn't nothing, but the something that he was no longer interested them. They wanted to move on, embark upon the journey again; and in this they were right. But they were wrong to pretend that the journey with Celtic Swing had never happened, to desecrate the memory of that sublime victory in the Racing Post Trophy by calling it 'a romp through the Doncaster mud', to forget that his public had once believed him to be an earthly Pegasus. The horse deserved better than that. He had been the inspiration for our magical dreams; it was not his fault that he had failed to fulfil them. And it did not mean that both the dream and the reality were not, in their separate ways, worth a great deal.

I still wonder now, though, at their difference from each other. I still think of the joyful simplicity with which the two-year-old Celtic Swing had pounded away from the field, compare it with the straitened, anxious finishes of his two classic races, and think: what happened?

There are the logical explanations. That he was an advanced two-year-old, pushed out to win by the greatest possible distance, against opposition that was still immature. That he did not improve, whereas other two-year-olds did. That the fast ground of the 1995 summer did not suit his stride and conformation. That he was not – and this was an argument that was to gain credence later in the year – entirely fit during his three-year-old season.

Then there are the other, more intuitive explanations. That the ease of his two-year-old victories, and of training gallops in which no other horse could keep up with him, had left him lazy. That his mind was not fully concentrated upon the severe task of winning classics. That he was a big, beautiful creature with powerful, indeed supernal speed, but without the lithe guile, the incisive edge of a true racehorse. That he was – and this is my instinct about Celtic Swing – a runner, not a racer.

It is something that can never be known, perhaps not even by his closest connections. The conundrum engaged the racing world throughout the summer, a time when, for all the retrospective speculation, one thing was certain, as certain as the faith in Celtic Swing had been. The quest for greatness was on again.

V

No two victories could have been more different than that of Celtic Swing in the French Derby, and that of Lammtarra, six days later, at Epsom. It was not simply that one ended a quest for greatness, and the other began one. It was that Lammtarra's Derby victory came from nothing and needed nobody. It was the purest victory I have ever seen.

If Celtic Swing had won by passing through the final furlongs in the way that Lammtarra did, there would have been fainting in the Grandstand. Bodies would have toppled from the Downs on to the course; top hats would have flown, like doves, into the air. Even if he had won in the way that he won the French Derby, there would have been a crowd response perhaps unprecedented at Epsom, for Epsom had been the expected scenario. But he was not there, on Derby Day 1995. Another horse, as unknown as Celtic Swing was known, won the race that we had believed to be his; and never was the detachment between crowd and spectacle made so clear.

This detachment is, as I have said, the natural state of affairs in flat racing. A supporter can urge his team to victory and even, by the force of his encouragement, impel it to score; but no spectator, however much they might have wished it, could have pushed Celtic Swing past Pennekamp in the Two Thousand Guineas.

The racing public knows this. It knows that it will never feel needed by the sport that it loves and, in accepting as much, achieves a dignified relationship with it: not so much a bond, more a respectful co-existence. But the public that comes to the big meetings – and they get no bigger than Epsom – is not used to this. It is used to sporting events at which the crowd has an active role to play: where it has sides to take, cheers and boos to allocate. And so the character of the big meetings, the Epsoms, the Royal Ascots, is very different from the relaxed, unified, egalitarian weekday meetings at Newbury or York. It is not just that they are bigger. They are something else altogether.

The Derby Day crowd, for example, is an entity with a life of its own, entirely separate from the race. Its relationship with the spectacle is not just detached. It is truly mysterious.

History has helped to give the crowd its identity, but accounts seem to suggest that it happened naturally and quickly. When the Derby was first run, in the late eighteenth century, it was a local affair attended only by a small crowd: perhaps five thousand at most. The connections of the horses would have been there and, swarming around them, would have been those whose interest was less legitimate. Corruption in racing was rife then. The sport may sometimes feel, now, like a law unto itself, but two hundred years ago it really was.

The institution of the Jockey Club, in around 1750, began to make a difference, especially when it made an example of George IV's (then Prince of Wales) jockey, Samuel Chifney, for pulling a horse. Nevertheless, it took a long while for the sport to be straightened out. Races were still pulled (as, indeed, they still are). In 1811, a man was publicly hanged for poisoning the water in a trough on Newmarket Heath; he had intended only to incapacitate the horses, but three of them died. In 1844, the Derby field contained a favourite that was deliberately pulled, a nobbled second favourite and two four-year-olds.

These early Derbies would, therefore, have disseminated an atmosphere both pure and impure: two opposing qualities would have filled the air with equal strength and equal insistence. The astringent, heady tang of this atmosphere, in which the purity of the contest itself pulls against the impurity that it creates, characterises all race meetings. The sound of galloping hooves is always shot through with the sharp shout of the bookmaker, the roar of the gambler. Nowhere, though, is this pull in the air felt so strongly as at the Derby: on that day, everything is extreme.

Throughout the nineteenth century, the crowds for the race grew with almost every year. Derby Day became established as one of the most important festivals in the English calendar: more fun than Easter, more purposeful than Christmas. There are several reasons for this increase in the popularity of flat racing, perhaps the most important of which was that newspapers began to carry race cards and results. Knowledge of the sport was thus spread beyond its hitherto tight circle. It also became better organised, enjoyed the joyful patronage of the Prince of Wales (and Lillie Langtry) and, with jockey Fred Archer and his five Derby victories, acquired a true sporting hero.

There was, too, an abundance of great horses: Voltigeur, who was bred in Hartlepool and won the 1850 Derby; Gladiateur, the Triple Crown winner of 1865, who was trained in France and known as 'the avenger of Waterloo'; Ormonde, who won the Triple Crown in 1886, and was Fred Archer's last Derby winner; La Fleche, a filly who won the 1892 Oaks and missed the Derby by three-quarters of a length; Persimmon, who won the 1896 Derby for the Prince of Wales; and, of course, the magnificent terror, St Simon. Flat racing was still, in its essence, what it had been and always will be: a sport truly accessible only to the few. However, the means to approach it were now there. And the Derby was approachable, to Londoners at least: the journey to Epsom was a short one, though the traffic jams were terrible. From before dawn, the road to Surrey thronged with carriages, broughams, hansom cabs and costermongers' carts, all of them crammed with people, whose Derby Day had already begun. Epsom was a common land course, as opposed to a park like Sandown: for those who spent the day on the Downs, rather than in a stand, attendance was free. And, of course, the race was run on a Wednesday, which meant sneaking a day off work. Everyone did it – throughout much of the nineteenth century, Parliament simply suspended itself – but there was still that delicious sense of truancy, that childish thrill of escape.

Descriptions of these Derby Days convey a Jonsonian quality: of the robust, hard-living city let loose, and set free, in a more spacious England, a place broad enough to encompass the whole nation. 'On the Derby Day,' wrote journalist George Augustus Sala, in 1892, 'London transports itself bodily to Epsom Downs . . . Belgravia jostles South Lambeth; Capel Court and Pall Mall rub shoulders; a contingent from Bermondsey comes down in the same train with a cohort from Highgate; all ranks and conditions of men and women are jumbled together on the course.' A powerful sense emanates from passages such as these, of a great crowd celebrating a great race. The crowd is shameless and vital in its impurity; the race is rigorous in its purity; but in some way the two go together, to make something peculiarly and splendidly English.

When I first went to the Derby, I had no expectations of the day. I knew about it, of course. My parents' racecards would be lying on a table – crumpled, marked with odd ticks, emblems of a larger world – as, on the first Wednesday in June, I would watch the news and see Snow Knight, then Grundy, then Empery, then The Minstrel, running up the Epsom straight to victory. From this I would catch a sense, even then, of the race as a part of England; and a sense of the Derby as the race upon which all else hangs.

When I finally participated in the occasion myself – a joyful, unforgettable day – I found that my impressions were remarkably

Lammtarra at Moulton Paddocks.

Celtic Swing at Angmering Park.

Ezzoud in triumph, winning the 1994
Coral-Eclipse Stakes at Sandown.

Ezzoud in disgrace, having thrown
Walter Swinburn at the start of the
1994 King George VI and Queen
Elizabeth Diamond Stakes.

Wonder horse no more: Celtic Swing is headed by Pennekamp (*left*) in
the 1995 Two Thousand Guineas.

Lammtarra's two trainers: Alex Scott (*above left*)
Saeed bin Suroor (*above right*).

The king colts of 1995: Godolphin's Lammtarra (*right*) and Halling exercise
on the gallops at Newmarket.

Lammtarra (green and white colours) begins to move through the Derby field: he made up more than six lengths in the final furlong and a half.

After the Derby: Lammtarra at the heart
of racing's inner circle.

Walter Swinburn, who thanked Alex Scott for guiding Lammtarra to his Derby victory.

Sheikh Mohammed, mastermind behind Godolphin Racing.

Lammtarra passes Tamure (maroon and white colours) to win the 1995 Derby. The winning time broke a record that had stood for nearly sixty years.

Lammtarra heads Pentire (*right*) to win the 1995 King George VI and Queen Elizabeth Diamond Stakes at Ascot.

The Queen congratulates Saeed bin Maktoum Al Maktoum, in whose colours Lammtarra ran, after victory in the King George.

Frankie's Leap.

Lammtarra races away from Swain and Freedom Cry (blue colours), towards victory in the Prix de l'Arc de Triomphe at Longchamp.

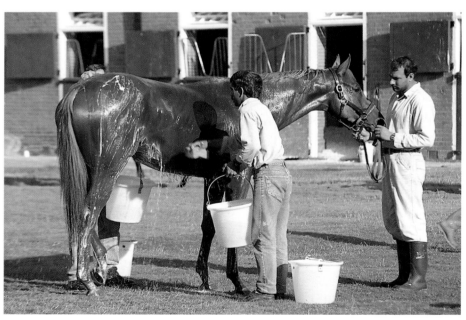

Lammtarra at Godolphin

similar to those of Sala; and of Dickens, when he wrote in 1851 that 'on Derby Day, a population rolls and surges and scrambles through the place that may be counted in millions.' One quarter of a million, more precisely – but the sense that Dickens conveys, of the presence of all England, is the right one.

That is how it feels. I felt it, from the moment of arriving on the platform for the train to Tattenham Corner, and standing amid the men in dogtooth checks and mafia sunglasses, with their bags full of lager and the *Sporting Life* wielded like a lance. I felt then the visceral joy, the bristling communality. I felt the luxury of the holiday, tautened by the sense of purpose. Through the lager and the smoke, I smelled the promise of the young summer, and the young horses. This was a race meeting, indeed.

On the walk from Tattenham Corner, I indeed found Ben Jonson's 'Bartholomew Fair': jellied eel stalls and big dippers and people carousing outside caravans, and car boots open to reveal boxes of Coke and Fosters and soft white rolls; bookmakers with ramshackle steps and boards, and men drunk at midday; and Gypsy Rose Lee, the fortune teller, whose planchette was poised to spell the name of the Derby winner.

Close to the Grandstand, the atmosphere became suddenly cleaner and tighter: Jaguars were being parked by men whose white shirts gleamed through dusky windows, and whose morning coats were stowed in cool, capacious boots. The chink of Members' badges could almost be heard as they unfolded themselves from their cars. With a smart tap, they adjusted grey toppers above faces exhausted with the strain of maintaining expressions of superiority, and glanced sharply around to make sure that everyone was looking at them. Then, closing off their faces again, they disappeared into the Enclosure.

The Enclosure was sealed off from the rest of the course by a high white wall, but all life congregated in the paddock before the Derby. The Queen was there. The grey toppers were there, as were the dogtooth checks. The middle classes, clutching their apologetic hats and pretending not to goggle at royalty, were there. The lycra miniskirts worn with the Salvador Dali wok hats were there. The horses were there, their heads nodding and tossing and a little strained, their bodies magnificently alive to the sun: the pure centre of this panorama.

It was a day such as I had never experienced, a piece of theatre in which everyone present was, simultaneously, actor and audience. It was a complex structure – rigidly stratified, yet rich with recesses and period detail – whose slender spire was the moment in which Generous passed the Derby winning post. I could not imagine that anyone with a sense of Englishness would not want to go to the Derby. I could not imagine that anyone with a feel for sport would not find, in the Derby, one of the year's most perfect moments. In the great crowd and the great race I found, not a single entity, but separate forces of comparable power.

That was in 1991, but since then the Derby has, according to popular wisdom, 'declined'. Saying as much started off as a fashionable opinion; now, as fashionable opinions will, it has become an unquestionable truth. The Derby has declined. It has lost its status, its glamour and its significance.

The reason for saying this seems to be that, whereas a quarter of a million people used to congregate in the Grandstand and on the Downs, now fewer than 100,000 do so. But the reason for this is surely obvious, and has nothing to do with the decline of the Derby. It is simply that sport has changed so much over the last few years, and never more so than in the years since Generous won the race.

Nowadays, although sport is more important than ever in people's lives, and commands ever more worshipping admiration, it is equally more accessible, more known, more answerable to its public. Its protagonists are at the mercy of their followers' whims.

Its great occasions are no longer events into which a crowd subsumes itself, willing to engage with something larger than itself; now, the crowd has its own self-conscious identity, its own importance. Hype, which used to be an optional extra, is now the marrowbone in the soup. People expect it; and they have come to want it, because it flatters them. You are worth selling to, says hype. You matter.

None of this, though, has much to do with the sport of flat racing, with its untouchable horses, its unfathomable jockeys, its remote gaze across an unchanging landscape. Sport is now sold on identification, on the insidious implication that those who watch and those who perform are soul brothers: wearing the same clothes, living the same life, separated by circumstances, united by inclination. But identification is somewhat hard to achieve with flat racing. You might admire Celtic Swing, but you cannot claim to be his soul brother.

This, to my mind, is what makes racing so unusually precious: that separateness, that silence. Even the hype of Celtic Swing retained a kind of purity about it, a true sense of awe (although the aftermath was tainted by cheap destructiveness: some of the press might have been writing about Paul Gascoigne). But, in a world where almost every human sport has such pervasive familiarity, animal sport cannot hope to compete. Quite simply, the Nike trainer angle is never going to be open to it.

Other reasons have been put forward to explain the 'decline of the Derby', but these are peripheral. It is irrelevant, for example, to say that moving the Derby meeting from BBC1 to Channel 4 caused a loss of prestige. The Channel 4 Racing programme is superb: its commentators have a quantity, and precision, of knowledge that other sports should envy. Betting expert John McCririck may remind one of Prince Monolulu, that silly old show-off who used to stand at the Derby in tribal costume, shouting 'Aahhh've gat a Haarse!', but John Francome and Derek

Thompson are repositories of racing wisdom. Viewing figures are lower than they were on BBC1: in 1995, 4.2 million people watched the Derby on Channel 4, compared with around six million in the late 1970s. But if viewers are really incapable of changing channels to watch the race, then one must assume that they were never particularly bothered about the Derby. One cannot blame Channel 4 for that.

And it is merely insulting to say that no Derby winners since, perhaps, Generous have captured the public imagination. Those horses had proud owners too; and why, anyway, does the public deserve to have its imagination captured? If it happens, it happens.

It is exactly this kind of thinking – oh my God, Erhaab won't interest the public, if only another horse had won the Derby! – that shows what is wrong with the Derby now. It is this reasoning which attributes, to the crowd, a significance beyond the event itself. Again, if it has that significance, it has it. If it loses it, it loses it. Such a thing can't be willed. Just because the Derby crowd disseminates an atmosphere peculiar to itself, and has a powerful independent life, that does not mean that this atmosphere, or life, can be created by anything *other* than the race. Yet this seems to be the idea. Talk about halting the 'decline of the Derby' seems to mean, quite simply, getting more people there. From that, goes the reasoning, everything will proceed: the rides at Bartholomew Fair will be full all day long, and the cheers, for the victory of a horse as popular as Celtic Swing, will be heard all the way back in London.

In the midst of all this, there is the race: diamond hard and pure. And the race does not decline. It is indestructible; the same race that it was in 1780. How can it be otherwise? It is the race in which, at the start, young horses stand upon the threshold of greatness; and, at the end, one of them passes through the door.

Federico Tesio, the Italian who bred Ribot, one of the greatest of them all, wrote this: 'The thoroughbred exists because its selection has depended not on experts, or technicians, or zoologists, but on a piece of wood: the winning post of the Epsom Derby.' No more rigorous test, in this most rigorous of sports, exists. Not only is the Derby horse running against the best that his year can offer – and it is almost always 'his', as for years now most fillies have contested the Oaks instead – but Epsom is a course that demands everything from him. Its mile and a half, which forms a loose horseshoe shape, requires him to round three bends and to handle merciless undulations.

Just to describe the Derby course fills one with awe. Its first five or so furlongs run 134 feet uphill. They round a slight right-hand bend, for which, obviously, a horse is best placed on the right of the course; then they swing quite sharply to start the first of its pronounced left-hand bends. The first 300 yards of this bend are on level ground. Then – as the commentators' famous phrase has it – 'they start the descent to Tattenham Corner', and run forty feet downhill in the space of only 300 yards. Finally, they round a sharper, second left-hand bend, before straightening up for the run-in of just under four furlongs. For much of this, the ground slopes gently downwards. Then, in the final hundred yards, it rises very slightly and pulls in left towards the winning post: both of these movements are tough on tired horses.

It is obvious from this that, to run the Derby course, horses need balance and agility. As my father puts it: 'Going round a bend while they're going downhill – they need five legs, really.' They also need the strength to run uphill and the conformation to run downhill. Celtic Swing is not the only horse to find this difficult: it is not something that racehorses, with their phenomenal speed and delicate legs, are meant to do. Although the downward slopes can make Epsom an easier mile and a half than, say, the stiff Irish Derby at The Curragh, they can also be very hard on some horses, especially when the ground is firm. As the sub-soil at Epsom is chalky, the course almost always has to be watered, either by nature or by design; 1995 was not unusual in this respect.

It is rare to find a Derby winner whose conformation is much less than perfect: even if they are small, like Erhaab and The Minstrel, they are beautifully formed. The horse will also need, in fairly equal parts, two qualities which tend not to be balanced against each other: stamina and speed. It will usually have done a certain amount of racing, because the Epsom fields are large, and of a remorseless competitiveness to frighten an inexperienced horse. And a Derby winner will be ridden by a jockey who can intuit the right way around the course, and the right moment to take the horse to the front. There are few of these, Piggott with his nine wins being the supreme example.

It is clear, from recordings of old Derbies, that some horses are defeated by Epsom. It saps them. Some, however, seem to thrive on it, gaining ever more strength from their mastery of its toughness, its trickery: they take the final furlong as if they have only just begun to gallop. Of course, these are not always the best horses in the field. Some Derbies are won by horses that are proved to be no more than good; though far more are won by the supreme horse of that year. But at the moment of passing the line – that most intense moment in the racing season – they are all great.

Often, it is only at that moment that they reveal themselves to be such. The Derby is a race full of secrets and surprises: for all their prior running, the abilities of its field are imperfectly known. Do they stay a mile and a half? None of them will have run that distance before. Do they run on good ground? Some of them may not have run in the summer before. How much speed, or desire, or guts have they got? These are things that, until now, can only be guessed: but the Derby will pull it all out of them, as surely as any National Hunt race. It cannot form a horse's reputation. Afterwards, he will be required to prove that his Derby win was no fluke. The rest of the season hangs upon the race, though; it is the phrase at the heart of the aria, to which the singer returns again and again. The Derby is the big one.

And the straight at Epsom is one of the most evocative stretches of land in the sporting world. The race changes when it reaches it: after all the bumping, the shouldering, the tactics, the strategy, it becomes ruthless and absolute. From here, one horse will emerge from the shapes that have been formed, and take possession of these final furlongs.

The straight comes into my mind at an instant: my eyes travel down its familiar open angle, with the white fence to its right. I can see many horses running down the faintly sunlit green, towards the winning post. There are the barely imaginable early winners, like Diomed, known only from paintings of their statuesque, curving bodies with the stiff, cropped tails. There are the great champions of the nineteenth century, like Ormonde, known only from dusky photographs. Then the images become clearer: I can see Humorist, for example, the Derby winner that most compels my admiration and pity. He won the race by a neck in 1921, and was the bravest horse that ever did so. Two weeks later, his stable lad saw a stream of red flowing from under the door of his box, and found inside the horse dead from tuberculosis, the walls about him splashed with his blood, his upper ear still pricked. He had won the Derby on only one lung.

I can see Hyperion, the horse whose small skeleton (15.1½ hh) stands in the National Horseracing Museum; with his sweet nature and unlikely appearance he was, in 1933, perhaps the most popular Derby winner of the century. I can see the grey horse Mahmoud, who in 1936 set a hand-timed course record of 2 minutes, 33.8 seconds, which was not to be beaten for fifty-nine years. I can see Sea Bird II, who in 1965 made the Derby look too easy and won the race in a canter, like an athlete saving his energy for the final. I can see the late surge of Sir Ivor in 1968, whom at the end of his career Lester Piggott was to call his favourite horse. And then I see, in

1970 and 1971, the two emperor horses of my generation: Nijinsky and Mill Reef, running towards the line as if they had been born to do so.

There is Roberto, with the trickling blaze so like Celtic Swing's, pushed to victory in 1972 by Lester Piggott and by a bare inch. There, in 1977, is The Minstrel, the neat little chestnut with the white face and the four white socks, again sent to victory by Piggott. I see the slim, elegant head of Henbit, another brave horse: without slowing for a second, he changed his stride when he cracked a foreleg in the final furlong, and still won the 1980 Derby. And then I see Shergar in 1981, holding in his power until, three furlongs out, he goes to the front and simply gallops, gallops away from them all. The ten-length margin of his victory is the greatest in the history of the Derby.

There are the two beaten certainties: El Gran Senor, who lost by a short head to Secreto in 1984; and Dancing Brave, who did not quite travel through the whole of the field as Lammtarra was to do, and failed by half a length to catch Shahrastani in 1986. There is Nashwan in 1989, whose action was the most beautiful I have ever seen: so buoyant and rhythmic that his hooves seemed merely to swing across the ground. And then I see the Derbies that I attended. Their memory is indestructible, but I remember them less as an image, more as a sensation. I can feel, for example, the powerful assurance of Generous, as his great chestnut body crossed the line in 1991. I can feel the acceleration of Erhaab, looking so small and young as he moved smoothly through the field. And I can both feel and see Lammtarra: the silk and velvet chestnut with the sombre eye, and the green and white silks fluttering like my heart, who took possession of the straight in the most mysterious and spectacular way of them all.

These are the true images of Epsom. They are brave, and splendid, and great; and every year, like a miracle, they are recreated. How, after a victory like Lammtarra's, can it be said that the Derby is in decline? If he had run it to an empty Grandstand, as he almost seemed to do, it would still have been what it was.

The essential unimportance of the Epsom crowd was revealed a long time ago, in 1972, when Roberto won the Derby under Lester Piggott. There had been controversy because another jockey had lost the ride; exaggerated and inaccurate rumours had abounded of Piggott's ungentlemanly conduct. When, therefore, Roberto was led into the winners' enclosure, he was met by the crowd with a murmuring silence. To see this on film is a painful thing: the horse, as the noble commentator Peter O'Sullevan says, 'did not deserve this', and to see the quietly victorious nods of his head, stubbornly unacknowledged by the ring of spectators, is quite unbearable. But the reality, of course, was different. While the crowd, with its self-righteous reaction to Roberto, was showing that it cared less for the greatness of the horse than for a display of its own pompous feelings, Roberto was showing the absolute stupidity of a crowd that expects a horse to comprehend disapproval. If the crowd cared little for the horse, the horse cared infinitely less for the crowd.

Racecourse Holdings Trust, which bought the owners of Epsom, United Racecourses, in 1994, did not see it that way. Its pledge to the Derby was that its crowd would grow, and 'the decline' would thus be halted. The race, after all, could look after itself.

In 1995, a three-year sponsorship deal was signed with Vodafone, worth £3.5 million to the Derby meeting. The prize money for the winning owner of the 1995 Derby would be more than £500,000 (Diomed, in 1780, won 1,125 guineas), and the prize money for the supporting cards would be greatly improved, with no race being worth less than £15,000. Racecourse Holdings Trust was also optimistic of increasing its television revenues, which in 1994 totalled £4 million. It planned to continue with changes to the racecourse, which included spending £200,000 on a paddock to be used only for the Derby meeting.

This was all very fine; but none of it would make much difference to the number of people who attended. Bearing in mind the revenue from sponsorship and television, getting a few more people to the course would not seem to matter much, especially as most of these would be sitting on the Downs and paying no entrance fee to the Grandstand. But that was not the point. The crowd must grow, not for purely financial reasons, but for the sake of the Derby: for the tradition of 'the Epsom crowd'.

So the decision was made to move the Derby from Wednesday to Saturday. It was the single, simplest and stupidest step that could have been taken, calculated most precisely to have an effect exactly opposite to the one that had been intended: that of reviving the atmosphere of Derby Day. It was unbelievable. I want to scream when I think about it (1996 will be even worse when, like any old first race at Kempton Park, the Derby will be run at 2.30 to accommodate the European football championships). The move to Saturday was a decision typical of the late twentieth century, with its marketing men who treat everything in the same way – as a commodity – and to whom individuality, character and tradition are as nothing. And institutions, even ones as great as the Derby, accept this. They too are in the late twentieth century, and know that what they are must be measurable in pounds sterling, column inches and crowd numbers.

The one thing that could, nowadays, have preserved the atmosphere of Derby Day was the fact of it being a Wednesday. This is not just because of the delicious air of escape that permeated the whole day – as if we had all skipped double maths and we had *all* got away with it – imbuing adult pleasures with a childish ecstasy. It is because, in order to sneak this Wednesday off work, a decision had to be taken: whether to do the proper, conscientious thing or whether to think: No. Sod it. I'm on the train to Tattenham Corner, with all the people who feel the way that I do, for a gorgeous dirty holiday, for drink and cigars and a pony on the dark horse outsider, and for the greatest race in the world.

On a Saturday, such a decision does not have to be taken. There is no effort required. There is simply a day, waiting to be filled. And so the Derby crowd of 1995 comprised people – all too many of them – who were there not because they chose to be at the Derby, but because they had to be *somewhere*. Epsom had become like one of those vast shopping malls within which people can now spend their lives: eating, spending, having their clothes dry-cleaned, putting their children on mechanical horses. There is no purpose to these places. They are simply somewhere to go.

To do this to the Derby was a terrible thing. But, to marketing men, a crowd is a crowd is a crowd. Saturday is the day on which crowds are formed, and so Saturday was the day which gave the Derby its best chance of getting a crowd. The fact that it would be a crowd as artificially built as if, in the race itself, the horses were made of plastic and silicon, did not seem to register. It did not matter who went to the Derby, so long as there were plenty of them: spending money and creating atmosphere.

In fact, the move to Saturday failed even in the way that it was meant to succeed. At the Oaks meeting, on Friday, the crowd was 8,000, and touts were selling £50 seats for the Derby at £30. The next day, the number of paying customers was indeed slightly up on 1994, at 23,497. But at 54,266, the crowd as a whole was not much more than half what it had been the year before. World Cup rugby and a test match had, as might have been predicted, claimed its attention. As might also have been predicted, the move to Saturday made corporate entertaining less convenient, and except for Vodafone few businesses attended the Derby. Perhaps most importantly of all in financial terms, betting turnover was down on the day, by an estimated twenty per cent on the £30 million of 1994. These figures may be even worse in 1996. The grip of the National Lottery upon our loose change seems to grow ever tighter: people who would, once, have had a pound or two on the Derby will now, perhaps, prefer to buy another couple of lottery tickets — especially on the day that the draw is made.

The move to Saturday also failed the Derby in other, less quantifiable ways. The Epsom crowd has always been full of people who know nothing about what they are watching: I have been one of them, and still loved the day. Not knowing, and even not caring, do not matter as long as they come with a willingness to enjoy and respect. But in 1995, there seemed to be people within the crowd who didn't just *not know*, or even just *not care*. They seemed, instead, defiantly intent upon showing that knowing and caring meant nothing.

It was, indeed, the strangest racing crowd I had yet encountered. It looked the same as ever, the same as when I first went to the Derby in 1991, but it struck me quite differently. It felt so disparate, so uncontrolled, so wilful. Its impurity was not that of smoke and drink and gambling, those warmly human venial sins; but of a wayward desire to impose itself upon the Derby.

I had not felt this before. The Epsom crowd had always asserted its own identity, but it had at the same time respected that of the Derby, whose power seemed to confirm that of its spectators. Though not in communion, the crowd and the race had been in balance with each other. Now, I felt the desire to tip this balance. I heard it in the meandering shouts, saw it in the drunken lurches, intimated it from the eyes turned inwards: not just indifferent, but unseeing. And I feared, irrationally, for the purity of the race. I could not stop thinking that the horses belonged to a world which no longer had a place here. Their vulnerability seemed acute: those proud necks, those etiolated legs, those separate and noble heads. What had they to do with this late-twentieth-century world, created at Epsom today: so wild yet so circumscribed, endowed with every means to enjoy itself except memory and imagination?

Everything had seemed all right when I arrived. I came early to the Derby, unable to wait any longer for the day to begin, and inside the Nashwan Bar in the Grandstand were just a few, desultory men, standing relaxed but alert to the pleasures that were to come. The air was already faintly blue with smoke, already echoing with rich laughter, already beginning to hum and throb and rev. I felt at home then. I had my drink, my cigarette, my *Sporting Life*. I had the understanding, appreciative nod from the men. I felt the race nudging continually at my propped elbow, alarming and delicious as the presence of a beautiful boy in a nightclub. I felt within me the presence of Nashwan himself, his rhythmic action swinging through my head with the wine. I was very, very happy. Less than an hour later, the bar was filled to the point at which my *Sporting Life* had to be folded into the size of a hymn book, and smoke had to be blown vertically, as if up a chimney. Yet the close sense of purpose remained: not spoken, not even necessarily comprehended, but infinitely powerful.

Outside the Nashwan Bar, this atmosphere disintegrated. It should have been massed in the air, as thick and pungent as the rounded puffs from a Cuban cigar; instead it seemed to trail and fall, as from the smouldering fag-end of a Craven A. As the day progressed, it should have become deeper and more intoxicating. Instead it became ever more dispersed: collecting occasionally in fierce hot heaps, more often drifting in spectral threads.

Yet everything *looked* the same. There were the grey toppers; there the jaunty trilbys; there the embarrassed middle-class straws; there the Salvador Dali woks; there the baseball caps – all present and correct. But because the idea of attending Derby Day for a reason – however imperfectly understood – had been taken away from much of this crowd, so the reason for the role-playing had gone.

In 1991, the fact that everyone present at Epsom was acting a part, as if in a Great Exhibition whose theme was The English Character, had seemed to me enchanting and humorous in the way that the English can be. I knew that the men in dogtooth checks were not really devilishly shrewd gamblers with pockets full of unkoshered money. I knew that the men in grey toppers were not really Lord Snooty. I knew that the lycra miniskirts were not really cocktail waitresses at The Happy Hour in Hainault – or, if they were, that was not all that they were. They were human beings, as well as caricatures. It was something about the occasion, the tradition, the place, the horses, the Englishness, that made us all want to play those parts. It was a joke, but it was also an affirmation. It was done with joy, and it was done with respect for Derby Day.

Now, though, there seemed to be something almost dangerous about the role-playing. If Derby Day was simply somewhere to go on a Saturday, what was the point in going there dressed as Slasher Green or Burlington Bertie? It wasn't funny, it was meaningless. And, if it was meaningless, it was therefore extremely meaningful: if there was no reason at all for prancing around a course, dressed as something out of the Great Exhibition, the fact that it was still being done gave to these class-ridden stereotypes an embittered significance. The joke was over, but the point of it remained.

The class structure that is implicit in the structure of the race-course had become horribly significant. The crowd wasn't just dressed as class stereotypes; it was acting the parts for real. The non-members were swearing and shouting, wrenching the rings out of lager cans with vicious force, stripping off their shirts as if daring the sun to scorch them. One of their girls, who was so drunk that she had begun to unbutton her suit, stumbled across the invisible electric fence that separated the Grandstand from Members'. 'Rosie!' screamed her boyfriend. 'Fucking get back here! You can't go in there, you silly cow! You'll get banged up!'

Meanwhile, the members were staring at Rosie as if she were a seaside donkey that had infiltrated the parade of Derby entrants in the paddock. Their eyes were cold, full of conscious superiority. They were in, she was not, and they were loving it. That was the

way they wanted it. Every time I fell amongst their rigorous tail-
coats and the elliptical resonance of their squeak and bray, I felt
diminished, down-at-heel, common as muck. Every time I emerged from their territory into the miasma of the Grandstand,
with its smell of frying fat and its angry, ribald sounds, I felt like the
Countess of Derby. Both feelings were absurd. Both were real.

What was so ridiculous was that, in everyday circumstances, neither set of people would have conducted themselves in this way.
But there was something here that was having an almost fatalistic
effect: turning the crowd into parodies of their class, as if there was
no other way in which they could behave. You think we're hoi
polloi? Right, mate, we'll give you hoi polloi. Upper class? Yes, you
common little man, certainly we are upper class.

This kind of behaviour always threatens at big race meetings,
with their apartheid system of segregation. There is something
about the sport itself which seems to generate it. The sphere that
it inhabits is so remote, after all; only the élite can breathe its rarefied air. The rest must live in a different world entirely, and the
big race meetings reflect this, with their enclosures and badges
and dress codes, their absolute definitions of who is in and who
is not. The snobbishness of the sport reflects it too: some of the
people who live and work within flat racing are intent upon
proving that they belong to the élite, the sphere of the thoroughbred. It is, perhaps, inevitable that the innate refinement of the
sport, the truly aristocratic nature of the horse, should be imitated by its followers – though as a mirror image it is distorted
and parodic.

It is a joke, again, of a particularly English kind. Only the fact that
it is a joke saves it from being repulsive; and at Epsom in 1995 it
ceased, for me at least, to be funny.

I was tired by the time of the Derby itself. I was exhausted with
walking back and forth from my seat to the ghastly new paved

paddock – stuck on the side of the course like a Texas Homecare carpark – and trying to follow the drifting threads of the day. As I approached the paddock once more, for the emergence of the Derby field, a part of me thought: let's get it over and done with.

Then how ashamed I felt, at the sight of the first horse, and the slow, calm sound of his hooves upon the stone. Thank God, I thought, for the absolute purity of this moment: for the indestructible ability of these horses to uplift me, to make me yearn towards beauty and nobility and mystery. Gratitude, as well as awe, filled me as one by one they made their entrance to the paddock. As humans we were wasting this day, grappling within it for excitement and thrills and satisfaction; but they were assured of their purpose, confronting the most important race of their lives, submitting with dignity to its merciless judgement.

There was Pennekamp, a very short-priced favourite by now, his name on his blanket too simple a signifier of what he possibly represented: the finest horse of his year. There was Spectrum, who carried my money. There was the classically handsome Presenting. There was the chestnut with the air of suppressed bewilderment, of unwilling perfection, whose vivid coat seemed at odds with his low, almost grieving head.

Lammtarra was 14–1 at the start of the race. He was the sixth most fancied horse in a field of fifteen: by now it was remembered that he had shown much promise as a two-year-old and that – like Moonshell, who had won the Oaks the day before – he had had the advantage of wintering in Dubai. But only one horse this century had ever won the Derby in his second race, and Morston, in 1973, had at least run his other contest as a three-year-old. What Lammtarra was attempting was damn near unprecedented.

Walking with him in the paddock were all the others whose fate, like his, I now know so well – the successes like Riyadian and Fahal, who would end the season in the Champion Stakes at Newmarket; the relative failures like Maralinga and Korambi, who would end it in the lowly races of the all-weather tracks; and the tragedy, Daffaq, who would stagger to the end of the Derby with an injury that would end his life – but who, during the moments when they circled beneath the young summer sun, glimmered no less strongly than Lammtarra with the possibility of greatness.

Perhaps appropriately to the atmosphere of this strange day, the 1995 Derby was a rough and ruthless race. From the moment that the stalls opened, it was run hard and fast: Daffaq, who was there for no reason but to set the pace for Munwar, was able to do so for only a few brief seconds. The leaders were Maralinga and Robert Sangster's Court of Honour, with Fahal and Riyadian also towards the front. Lammtarra was reasonably placed as they climbed the hill and rounded the first, right-hand bend. 'I had had orders,' says Walter Swinburn, 'to keep in the first three or four all the way. But I thought that would be impossible.'

As, indeed, it proved to be when the race swerved to the left and Lammtarra, 'through no fault of his own', got cut off. Maralinga and Court of Honour were still the leaders, with Presenting running smoothly behind them, Munwar well-placed on the rails and Pennekamp, it seemed, perfectly poised on the outside. Lammtarra, Spectrum and Daffaq ran in a line towards the back of the field, the position of all three worsening as the race moved downhill and curved again to the left. As he rounded Tattenham Corner, Lammtarra was adrift in that place where those with no hope in the Derby collect, one by one, as the race and its leaders progress; at that moment it seemed as though, for all his perfection, he was fated to be an unlucky horse.

Coming into the straight, it seemed impossible that he should even be placed, but Swinburn was 'lucky enough to remember what horse I was on'. He started to move hard on Lammtarra, urging him with all his tiny body to open that vast store of power. In front of him the field was starting to lengthen, with Court of Honour and Presenting still towards the front, Frankie Dettori's mount, Tamure, moving up and Pennekamp still poised. Behind him Spectrum was making no ground at all, while Daffaq was moving further and further backwards. Lammtarra was holding a position on the rail behind Munwar, in which he was avoiding trouble but was also becoming increasingly trapped: 'That wasn't my biggest worry, though, that the gap would appear. It was more that I was too far off the pace.'

Three furlongs out, it became clear that Epsom had defeated Pennekamp: he was still holding his position poised on the outside, but his galloping no longer seemed to be taking him forwards. The focus of the race shifted remorselessly away from him, up the field, towards a group of horses that was stretching away from the rest. Fahal was there, with Presenting, Court of Honour and Tamure, all going well; some way back were Munwar and Vettori, with Lammtarra yet further behind. And then the gap did appear for Lammtarra: two furlongs out, he moved out from behind Munwar. In doing so he bumped him and, in turn, Munwar bumped Vettori; this occasioned a stewards' inquiry after the race, which found the interference to have been accidental.

Lammtarra's movement out to the centre of the course seemed to take a long time. For several precious seconds, he seemed to travel sideways while the horses in front pulled further and further away from him. 'I was getting him well balanced. You have to wind him up, like in the race at Newbury. He hadn't started to motor yet.' With less than two furlongs to run, Fahal was clear of Tamure at the front, but Tamure looked ominous on his outside. How surprising, I remember thinking, that of Sheikh Mohammed's two runners, he, not Pennekamp, should be about to win the Derby; with a hundred yards to the line, he powered past Fahal with a surge that seemed decisive. In almost any other Derby, it would have been. It was simply that, this year, down the centre of the Epsom straight a horse was running another, greater race of his own.

'From three furlongs out, my hopes got better and better. One furlong out, I thought that I would win. People who want to crab Lammtarra say they were stopping in front – they weren't. He put in an astonishing performance in those last furlongs. And that horse knew exactly what was happening. He only does what is required of him, but he will dig deep.'

Lammtarra made up more than six lengths in the last furlong and a half of the Derby. He passed Tamure in the final, fleeting instant and beat him by a whole length; Presenting, who had passed Fahal at the same moment, was three-quarters of a length behind in third. This meant that Lammtarra, unlike Erhaab the year before, had flown past two horses whose ability to stay a mile and a half was beyond doubt. Behind Fahal, in fifth, was Court of Honour; Vettori, who had run a fine and difficult race, was sixth. Lammtarra's Derby winning time of 2 minutes 32.31 seconds beat the record of Mahmoud, which had stood for fifty-nine years, by a second and a half.

I have watched the recording of this 1995 Derby more times, now, than I can count. Every time, before I do so, I am filled with a kind of reluctant fear, as if I am about to hear a piece of music which disturbs as much as it brings joy. Familiarity makes no difference. In fact, it remains impossible simply to *watch* the race: it compels me to engage with it, to give it the whole of my attention and my emotions.

Every time, as the field rounds Tattenham Corner, I say to myself, no – he can't do it. Every time, as Lammtarra moves sideways in the straight and hangs there, calmly suspended, while the race powers further and further away from him to its climax, I say: Go forwards! Go forwards – you'll never make it! And then I hear the catch in the voice of the commentator – 'Lammtarra's coming from another county' – and I sense the movement of the horse, surging through me like life itself, its power never lessening. The thing that I know will happen meets the thing that, every time, I cannot believe will happen; and I feel myself quicken like a flame as I watch Lammtarra win the Derby, yet again.

It was not a joyful Derby. The emotions it compelled were beyond that: they were harsh, painful and ambivalent. A few long moments after Lammtarra passed the winning line, after Tamure and Presenting and Fahal and the others whom the race had glorified, came those whom it had destroyed. There was Pennekamp, his potential greatness wrecked for the season, perhaps for ever, by a fractured fetlock joint. There was the injured Maralinga. There was Spectrum, also injured, not to run again until September. And there was Daffaq, lunging sideways as, still trying as hard as he was able, he galloped down the straight. His knee was fractured. Later on Derby Day he was put down.

And what of the emotions aroused by Lammtarra's victory? What of those people who had known the horse as a two-year-old, before he was propelled into such fantastic and sudden stardom? What of those who had known Alex Scott, the man who had dreamed of the events of this day? David Phipps, who had been Scott's head lad, watched the Derby at his home, in the grounds of the stables where Lammtarra had lived. 'I backed him in the Derby. I had some of Alex's bet. And the day of the Derby, I sat here and thought – he can't do it. I knew how ill he'd been. Godolphin said he was well in himself, they were pleased with him. But I thought – can he do it? . . . It was great to see him win. But it was sad, in a way, because of the situation.'

Julia Scott was also watching the Derby at home. It is very hard to imagine her feelings as Lammtarra, the horse in whom her husband had believed so strongly, won the race for which Scott had backed him the previous summer. That bet now was hers: making an appropriately gentlemanly gesture, Ladbrokes had waived the rule that a wager dies with the man who strikes it.

'I felt pretty numb after the Derby. I mean, it was so ghastly with everything that had happened – it was almost like the final straw, really. Because you just imagine what would have been. The only way I was happy was that Alex's judgement had been vindicated. But then that just made it more sad, really . . . I suppose I'd rather he'd won than been a close second.'

Walter Swinburn spoke movingly of Alex Scott after the race. His voice, quiet and precise despite the Tannoy, formed a point of concentrated dignity amid the frenzy. 'Coming down the hill I said "Please God, please Alex, give me daylight," and it was like Moses and the Red Sea opening up . . . I know he was helping me from above . . . I did believe in God beforehand, but I really do now.'

Sheikh Mohammed, who assumed command of Lammtarra in the winners' enclosure while his nephew, in whose colours the horse ran, watched the race in Dubai, said: 'To get this horse here, and see him win, has given me more pleasure than winning four Derbies in my own colours.' For him, and the Godolphin operation, it must have been a proud and remarkable moment. But he said, too, that 'it would have been a much happier day for me if Alex Scott had been here.'

By the end of Derby Day, the straight at Epsom – that most evocative stretch of turf – seemed to be shadowy with ghosts. Real ghosts, not just memories. There was Daffaq, five minutes earlier circling the paddock within a sunlit haze of possibility, now lurching pitiably across the winning line. There was Lammtarra, flying towards victory, the power of his achievement bringing an equivalent intensity to the tragedy of Alex Scott.

Yet his race, when he ran it, held none of this. As I have said, it was the purest victory I have ever seen. The sense that Lammtarra came from nowhere and needed nobody is, of course, an illusion; just as it would have been an illusion, had Celtic Swing won the Epsom Derby instead, to feel that he was the creation of a public who had willed his victory. Those who knew Lammtarra before

Derby Day – David Phipps, Julia Scott, Sheikh Mohammed, Walter Swinburn – had, of course, helped him to achieve greatness. But when he did it – when he lengthened his lean, bright body, and put down the head with its sad, strong, impersonal eye, and ran past Pennekamp and Spectrum and Munwar and Vettori and Presenting and Fahal and Tamure, all the ones who might have been, and entered his own world of speed and triumph – then he was alone. 'Oh God, I must congratulate you,' I said to Walter Swinburn, when I met him two weeks afterwards at the final of the Greyhound Derby, 'it was the most extraordinary thing I ever . . .' 'Ah, no,' he said, with polite sincerity. 'You should congratulate Lammtarra.'

I held the sensation of that final furlong within me as, after the last race, I returned to my car. Around me the disturbed and destructive day reverberated. The cold eyes beneath the grey toppers seemed indifferent to the ghosts of Daffaq and Scott; the drunkenness on the Downs seemed to mock them. 'Fucking hell, look what we've got here,' said a group of men, leering and tumbling into my path as I walked the darkening road from the course. On another Saturday, three months later, they might have been at Millwall football ground; they should not have been at the Derby. As I tried to evade them I clung to the thought of Lammtarra, which curved inside me like a rose stem. As they continued to shout, I thought how impossible it was that he had been watched by men like this. How could the purity of Lammtarra's Derby, and the impurity of theirs, be part of the same world?

They could not. They had shared a span of time, and an acreage of ground, but nothing else. The differences between them were visible and absolute: the thoroughbred versus the yob; the horse who had penetrated the mystery of greatness, against the men who dared not even consider the existence of that mystery. But they were differences that I felt, within myself, as I drove away from Epsom. I held Lammtarra to my heart, to my very being. I pressed the thought of his victory as if I would extract its vital juice, trying to make its fleeting moment a part of my whole life. It had given me such pleasure, such intensity of emotion; but I knew that it could not be held, that it flew free of me. Even the memory of it would not really be mine, but part of that remote and mysterious world which it inhabited.

My feelings reminded me of a visit to Ancient Rome: standing at night in the Capitol, the lights of the city behind me, staring into the glancing eye of Marcus Aurelius's horse. If I wanted this sight to satisfy me, I thought, I would have to stand here for the rest of my life. When I leave it, I cannot take with me what this moment holds. The only consolation is the knowledge that I can return, and enter the moment again.

VI

I WAS NOT THE ONLY person left a little stunned by Lammtarra's Derby. Opinion was united on the fact that running the race on Saturday had been a terrible idea; beyond that, no one knew quite what to say. It was as if the horse, when he passed the post, had cannoned into the entire racing public at the same time and knocked it sideways. How could he have been so remarkable and so unexpected? How *could* he have won like that, breaking the Derby course record, when he had run a single race ten months earlier, and had nearly died ten weeks ago? Was it the winter in Dubai? Was it a poor Derby field? Was it a fluke? What if Pennekamp had not injured himself? What if Celtic Swing had run? What would happen when Lammtarra ran again?

So many questions without pre-prepared answers – it was a relief for the racing season to turn, ten days after the Derby, to Royal Ascot. No Lammtarra, no Pennekamp, no Celtic Swing. After the agonies and shocks of the Two Thousand Guineas and the Derby, Ascot soothed like balm. And it was bliss in 1995: the best I have ever known.

Sun is everything at Royal Ascot. It takes the components of the day – the racing, the clothes, the wanderings, the champagne, the picnics – and wraps them in a warm and infinitely glamorous veil. The light falls lovingly upon everything: the coats of the horses, the sparkling glasses, the bright peacock dresses, the smiles beneath hat brims. In 1994, wind had swirled around me as, after the day's racing, I had crouched on a seat of my father's car, hat bumping against the roof, heels sticking out the side to make the pretence that I wasn't, actually, *inside*. The wind was bringing with it vicious little flurries of rain; but I had clung with icy hands to my glass of champagne and plate of food, and to my stalwart determination that, after the racing at Royal Ascot, there would be a picnic. The absurdity of it hovered dangerously. The weather had made every-thing pointless: the flimsy suit, the hat that necessitated walking around with one hand permanently on top of the head, the straw-berries and wine eaten half in, half out of the car. Why, I thought, didn't I just stand all day in a big sensible coat, with a hipflask in its pocket and binoculars slung about its lapels, and watch the bloody racing?

The next year, though, when the days of Royal Ascot were sen-sually hot, everything acquired the same sharp dazzle and came back together again. I wandered from paddock to Tote to en-closure: all that to and fro which, on less unified days, can seem a pointless mockery of the routine that I am supposed to be escaping, but which, within that slow and hazy atmosphere, became dense with energy. I felt real joy in the sight of the gleam upon horses' necks, upon green turf, upon raised glasses, upon clothes that had been planned with such care. I was at Ascot for much of that week, driving from Berkshire to London with a bare arm hanging out of the car window, between the charged relaxation of the course and the febrile thrill of the greyhound Derby heats. It was one of the best weeks I have ever had.

Royal Ascot, like Epsom, is a big meeting, and so, again, there is much mutual indifference between crowd and event. Women stand in the Ladies' spearing their heads with hat-pins while, outside, can be heard the trundle and shout of some of the most important races of the season. Men queue at the bars beside the course, laughing amongst themselves, as the horses gallop past them – they can always watch the race afterwards on the telly screens. Crowd and event are both doing what matters to them. Neither is affected by the indifference of the other.

As at Epsom, the crowd has an identity of its own, with a power comparable to that of the event. And again, in a way that can hardly be explained, that identity derives from the event, however much it remains separate from it. The Ascot and Epsom crowds are similar; or, at least, they were until Epsom started believing the self-fulfilling prophecy of its 'decline'. Above all, they are both English crowds. They are both drawn to the big race meetings by English notions of tradition and class, of the countryside and horses, of sport and good times. They are drawn, too, to play a part on these occasions: to affirm their connection with their past and their country by wearing it, parading it, proving it to themselves as they display it to the crowd.

Like Epsom, Royal Ascot is a Great Exhibition, but the atmosphere of the exhibition is quite different at the two meetings; and this, too, derives obscurely from the event itself. Royal Ascot does not have the obvious *purpose* of Derby Day. Epsom, after all, contains the race upon which so much of the subsequent season will hang; its outcome has an absolute significance, and this gives to the day a kind of taut, narrow-eyed alertness. The Royal Ascot races, on the other hand, are merely prestigious. To win one is an honour to a horse, but it does not define its reputation; nor is any one of these races a great deal more important than the rest. The Queen Anne Stakes (named after the splendid woman who commissioned the building of Ascot, and used government funds to supplement the prize money), the St James's Palace Stakes, the Gold Cup, the Coventry, the Wokingham: they come in large, steady, rhythmic waves, rather than as a single tsunami erupting through a calm but imminent sea.

So, by comparison with Epsom, the atmosphere of the Royal Ascot meeting is easier, perhaps happier, certainly less intense. Without necessarily realising it, the crowd has absorbed the feel of the races, and adjusted its pitch accordingly.

Of course, as at any event which hopes truly to represent the English character, the apartheid system of class segregation is in place. It is defined by the presence of the Royal Family, by the ceremonial of their carriage drive down the course, and by the Royal Enclosure into which they 'invite' — a charming notion — those people who have been vetted by the system and allowed this privileged entry. The borders of the Royal Enclosure are patrolled by the Bowler Hat Brigade. These are racecourse officials, rather like characters in *Alice in Wonderland*, who spend the week staring at people's breasts and holding up their hands in unison when the wrong badge tries to gatecrash the right place.

I have attended Ascot both in and out of the Royal Enclosure. The difference, on these occasions, in the way that the Bowler Hats treated me was quite frightening. One year I was a painted trollop whose very presence might contaminate the dear Queen; the next year I was a charming young lady who clearly knew that the milk goes in second. But so fantastically, so openly snobbish are the Bowler Hats, that they serve the important purpose of reminding one that, every year, the great race meetings are telling a great, English joke. Into the Enclosure go the Lord Snootys; out into the hinterland beyond go the dogtooth checks and thigh-length flamenco dresses. At Royal Ascot, it seems funny, absurd and, somehow, not offensive. To say as much may sound patronising and complacent but, for this week at least, everyone seems happy to be where they are: savouring their position amongst the buttoned morning coats, having fun amongst the loosened ties. To take exception to the system would, I think, miss the point of Royal Ascot.

At Epsom, one rubs against the bristle of raw power — that surging, uncontrollable crowd, that rough race with its almost alarming sublimity – and the day has a great, dirty grandeur about it. Royal Ascot, by comparison, is controlled, highly ordered: almost Toytown. If the big city does come to it, then as soon as it enters the course it is mysteriously emasculated. Indeed, the male feel of Epsom, with its smoke smell and rumbustious noise, is almost completely diluted at Royal Ascot: women, here, are the dominant sex. They take possession of the week with their carefully-packed hampers, full of delicacies and proper cutlery; with their picnic furniture, ranged proudly around the carparks; with their tea breaks between races; and, above all, with their clothes.

This is, perhaps, the one week of the year upon which a man will not disown a woman who has gratified the desire, buried at all other times, to disguise herself as the fairy inside a musical box. Instead he will take her arm, gaze upon her proudly, smile indulgently as she adjusts once more what she hopes to be the slice of smartness upon her head, which is wobbling like a bit of blancmange on top of a rugby ball. On Ladies' Day – a phrase I can hardly bring myself to write, so reminiscent is it of the between-song patter of provincial nightclub singers – the man suppresses his longing to be hovering around the bookmakers and drinking pints of lager. He buys champagne, his eyes gleaming as they try not to weep at the cost. He presents his woman with a metaphorical box of Milk Tray.

I know women for whom Royal Ascot is the highlight of the year. In January, they are buying their outfit in the sales; in February, they are reading recipes for guacamole; in March, they are stocking the freezer with canapés. It sounds silly, but it is also charming, for this is, as I say, a day dedicated entirely to pleasure: to arranging the props perfectly for a perfect day. Of course, perfect days don't necessarily happen because they have been planned. Royal Ascot needs the sun, for one thing. But there is a kind of determination in the way that such people march upon the week, even through rain and wind, teetering across the turf and holding on to their hats, that is indomitable, uplifting and, again, very English. When, a couple of years ago, I uncovered the purpose behind the meeting, and realised the importance of these races and horses, I became enraged, like a newly renegade smoker, with the unconverted and desultory crowd around me. 'Watch the bloody horses!' I wanted to shout. 'Leave the bloody hat and look at what's going on!' But, in 1995, I realised that I had been wrong to see aimlessness in the Royal Ascot crowd. I realise now that there is another purpose there, beyond the event itself: that of playing one's part in creating the perfect image of an English summer day.

Royal Ascot is not a place in which memories accrue. It is not Epsom, with that evocative straight and so many horses running down it towards greatness. Ascot is too bland, too easy for that: it simply happens, in the present, in the summer. When I think of it, I think of the sun throwing its veil of glamour over those English summer days, and over me as I move within them. That is all. It is lovely.

And so I felt, as I attended Royal Ascot in 1995, a smooth and comforting hiatus in the season's quest for greatness. For a short while, it was forgotten: after the Two Thousand Guineas and the Derby, it was time to enjoy the sport again, to savour the performances of fine horses without that compulsion to judge, to wonder and to hope. The hunger created by Celtic Swing was still unassuaged. Pennekamp might have filled it, but Lammtarra had not: he was too unexpected, too baffling. The Irish Derby, in which both he and Celtic Swing might run (Pennekamp was, of course, injured), was waiting for us in early July. Until then, however, we would relax in the sun, and watch the racing.

To my gratification, I found that my growing obsession with the racing season had increased my knowledge of the sport. When I came to study the race cards at Ascot, which I did with fascination but without the emotional involvement of the previous weeks, I felt as if my brain had been loosened by those concentrated exertions: almost without my realising it, it had grown able to recognise names, races, colours.

This was a pleasure that I had not looked for. So intense had been my gaze upon Celtic Swing and Pennekamp that I had not realised, until I saw it in the Royal Ascot race card, how easily I would recognise the name of Bahri, who had run behind them in the Guineas. Not only did I know him, I knew *about* him. I knew that he would be ridden by Willie Carson; that he wore the blue colours and striped cap of Sheikh Hamdan Al Maktoum; that he ran a mile as well as almost any horse in the country. With him in the race was Annus Mirabilis, whom I also knew about. I knew that he wore the maroon and white of Sheikh Mohammed, that he had finished twelve lengths behind Celtic Swing in the Racing Post Trophy, that this form meant, now, whatever anyone wanted to make of it. And then – I turned the page – Vettori. I knew his blue colours with the white chevron, those of Sheikh Maktoum, the eldest brother; I knew his fine run in the Derby; I knew that he had wintered with Lammtarra in Dubai.

Little scraps of information, adding up to almost nothing – I knew that too – but I was beginning to feel that I was moving, tentatively, through the world of this sport: that, although it was still a vast, remote and undiscovered country, I was able to pick out a sign here, a landmark there, to discern the occasional familiar shape within the expanses of green turf, across which ran so many mysterious horses. I no longer felt that I was running, blindly, through a sphere of memories and legends. I was treading, however timidly, the real terrain: tracing the infinite complexity of its patterns, perceiving the way in which they sometimes coalesced, sometimes dissolved.

My pleasure, in this sudden awareness of my awareness, became fierce when I recognised a name in the Prince of Wales's Stakes: Muhtarram. Muhtarram. How did I know it? I knew it, I knew it, but . . . then I remembered. A picture of the horse came to me quite clearly, his strained and open face bobbing beside the blinkered one of my beloved Ezzoud, in the final furlong of that race at York . . . the Juddmonte International. Muhtarram. The blue colours of Sheikh Hamdan again – Willie Carson again? Yes. I was becoming *au fait* with all of this: I was going to back the horse. I had my own, special memory of how he had battled against Ezzoud; I had my own, private opinion of how good a horse it took to stay with Ezzoud, as Muhtarram had done, when the masked man was in the mood to win. At six years of age, the oldest horse in the race, Muhtarram was carrying a lot of weight – nine stone eight – but he was also going to carry my money. Then I glanced across the page and saw the name of Balanchine.

I knew her too! I knew that she had been the finest horse of the previous year: the filly who had taken on the colts in the Irish Derby and destroyed them, in a way that fillies rarely do. I knew that she had nearly died; that, miraculously, she was here again; and that, here with her, was one of the conundrums that flat racing presents more often, and more completely, than any other sport. What was Balanchine about to do? Was she about to reclaim the form of 1994, when she had won two – almost three – classics with such strength and will? Or had she been subtly defeated by her illness, able to race again but not to conquer? The answer to the conundrum lay within her beautiful chestnut body. Nothing, nothing but the race itself would bring it to the light. Every horse, in every flat race, is capable of doing something that it has never done before. This example of Balanchine was simply an extreme illustration of her sport's essential, compelling elusiveness.

Now I was agonising over my fiver. I even gave consideration to another name – again, because I had recognised it: that of Eltish, whom I knew to have been a promising two-year-old in 1994, and to have run well in the Kentucky Derby the month before. The

119

other horses in the race I did not look at. It was difficult enough as it was.

In the end I backed Muhtarram – for no other reason than that I thought it best to stick to my first impulse – and, in the end, after a prolonged study of the photo finish, he was announced to have won the race from Eltish. Balanchine ran a distant fifth. That saddened me; but the victory gave me fierce pleasure.

It meant nothing, of course. Backing a horse because of some incomplete memory, entirely separate from the rest of his career and the rest of the field, is a meaningless act, but it gave me the illusion of mastery over that particular race, that particular tiny fragment of the sport. Muhtarram was the first winner I ever backed because of some glimmer, however faint, of true knowledge. He was the first winner that I truly owned.

This was a very different thing from backing Generous and Erhaab in the Derby, which I had done because my father told me to. *He* had owned those winners; I had not. At Royal Ascot, though, I watched the striped blue cap of Muhtarram through every moment of the race; and, for that brief couple of minutes, I felt that my fate was bound to his. He was not a horse that I could own, now or in any realistic future. Ours was a relationship that existed only in my heart. Nonetheless, my knowledge of him, and of the place that he occupied within the racing season, had – for a fleeting, delirious instant – brought that relationship to life.

He was my only winner at Royal Ascot. The second day presented another of flat racing's insoluble conundrums when, in the Coronation Stakes – a race for three-year-old fillies – Harayir, who had won the One Thousand Guineas, was pitted against Ridgewood Pearl, who had won the Irish One Thousand Guineas. Also in the race, incidentally, was Myself, whom Lammtarra had beaten in his two-year-old race at Newbury; and Gay Gallanta, who had beaten Myself at Royal Ascot the year before.

The Coronation Stakes, however, had been reduced to a bare

and essential question: which of the two Guineas winners would triumph? Had Harayir lost in Ireland because she disliked the soft ground? Had Ridgewood Pearl won because she loved it? Would she, therefore, dislike the firm turf of Ascot? Would Harayir relish it? Having seen her win the Guineas at Newmarket, and heard the simple awe in her jockey's voice as he said, 'When I asked her to go, she just flew,' I backed Harayir. Ridgewood Pearl won the race easily. There had been no way, in the world, of knowing whether she would run on the fast going, for she had never tried to do so before. But she did. I had guessed wrong. With her big, open gallop she reminded me a little of Celtic Swing; she had much of his power. She was to prove it again and again during the 1995 season.

Bahri, also, was to prove a good deal, as he intimated when he won the St James's Palace Stakes at Royal Ascot, pulling lengths away from Charnwood Forest and Vettori (my bet). Other interesting winners were Blue Duster, a two-year-old filly of Sheikh Mohammed's, with her impressive victory in the Queen Mary Stakes; Double Trigger, who won the two-and-a-half-mile Gold Cup, a race whose prestige has diminished with the increasing emphasis on speed rather than stamina, but which is still perhaps the most celebrated of the Royal Ascot meeting; and Pentire, who won the King Edward VII Stakes, known as the Ascot Derby. Pentire had won the Classic Trial at Sandown, but had not been entered for Epsom. He won at Royal Ascot in such a way as to make observers regret this absence.

Around this time, an interview was printed in the *Sporting Life* with Peter Savill, owner of Celtic Swing. In it he admitted his regret at not running his horse at Epsom; but he reiterated his certainty that his decision had been the right one. He could not, he said, have run that horse on that track and that going. The Derby, he went on to suggest, should be moved to the Friday of Royal Ascot.

Of course, it was inevitable that this suggestion met with some cynicism, attributing Savill's antipathy to Epsom to the fact that Celtic Swing was not built to run there. But the truth was that, in 1995, there had been other horses whom the course had defeated: Pennekamp, Spectrum, Maralinga, Daffaq. Was the Derby regarded as the greatest race, not just because the greatest horses so often won it, but because it was so hard and tough? Was it, in that sense, like the Grand National, a race that I had always loathed because of that very argument: that it was the ultimate test because so few horses could even pass it, let alone triumph in it?

When I thought of Daffaq, I was ashamed of my love for the Derby. I couldn't think of it as comparable with the Grand National, because that ghastly race carries with it the near-certain knowledge that horses will be injured, possibly killed. In the Grand National, tragedy is to be expected; in the Derby, it is a shock. But there was, still, that hint of similarity between the two races, that belief that the harder the better. Daffaq's death was an extremely unusual occurrence, and the number of injuries in the 1995 Derby were almost certainly caused by the ground: artificial watering is a poor substitute for rain, and Epsom had had none for a month. I knew this, and I knew, too, that what Peter Savill had said about the Derby was not more evidence of the race's 'decline'; as if, like the Royal Family, the Derby was now a tradition that people were constantly looking to criticise. Savill had spoken from the heart, not just on behalf of his own horse, but for those others who *had* run in the Derby, and whose owners now surely regretted this. What he said had to make one think.

My instinct was still towards Epsom, towards the straight that ran with memories, although amongst them also ran the real ghosts. I had hated what the move to Saturday had done to Derby Day, but I believed a return to Wednesday would restore it to what it had been before. I could not equate the power of the Derby with the ease of Royal Ascot. I felt that each might destroy the particular quality of the other.

After all – so my thoughts went – any animal sport carries with it a kind of guilt, a sense that people are making use of these horses and dogs for their pleasure. The guilt brought by Derby Day was perhaps no greater than that which any other day might bring. Yet to court guilt – to know that people have not done everything possible to protect these animals from harm – was something that worried me. It took flat racing into the realm of National Hunt, and made me a hypocrite for loving the one and hating the other. It gave literal, as well as metaphorical, power to Gericault's painting of the Derby, in which the horses seem to run in a kind of wild-eyed terror.

My cowardly conclusion was to wait and see what happened in 1996. If injuries of such severity and number occurred again, then the decline of Derby Day would no longer be a fashionable opinion, but a grim reality.

Another horse who had run in the 1995 Derby was injured during June and, as Peter Savill said in his interview: 'Who can say whether Lammtarra's injury originated there?' This, of course, was merely thinking aloud. The fact is simply that Lammtarra wrenched a joint in one of his hind legs two weeks after the race. Unable to train, he was withdrawn from the Irish Derby, which was run at The Curragh on 2 July and which, for recent Epsom Derby winners Nijinsky, Grundy, The Minstrel, Shirley Heights, Troy, Shergar, Shahrastani, Kahyasi, Generous and Commander in Chief, had been the arena of their subsequent triumph.

There had been no rain, but Celtic Swing was in the field for the Irish Derby. Three horses who had run at Epsom were there with him – Court of Honour, Munwar and Humbel – along with Godolphin's Classic Cliché, who had run second to Pentire at Royal Ascot. Presenting was to have run but, rather splendidly, he refused to get on to the aeroplane to Ireland.

I was in the USA when the race took place. In a way I hoped to be able to miss it. Nevertheless, I searched obsessively through the listings of the cable channels, eventually finding the Irish Derby within a Sunday afternoon racing programme. Much was made of the fact that the race was sponsored by Budweiser: cans of lager rolled continually across the screen. It was presented by a slick New Yorker, who announced each horse like the MC of an Atlantic City boxing match – 'And it's Cel-tic . . . Swiiing!!' – and by a sidekick dressed up as a joke Irishman, with a flat cap and a penny whistle, who echoed the words of his partner with a contrasting, complementary dying fall. 'Ah, Celtic Swing . . . to be shure.'

Watching the race in such circumstances, in the middle of a sultry afternoon in Greenwich Village, in the company of a cliché American and a comic who would have been booed off the stage in a nineteenth-century music hall, diffused some of the intensity that I would have felt back in England. Removed from its familiar context, the Irish Derby very nearly became just a race; Celtic Swing became, not quite so nearly, just a horse. I was glad of this, because an unfulfilled part of me was still yearning for his victory. By a length, by a short head – that no longer mattered. At the same time another part of me was feeling, with a sad and fatalistic certainty, that this victory would not come.

Celtic Swing was 5–4 favourite for the Irish Derby, but it was no surprise, somehow, when two furlongs out he seemed to stop. Like Pennekamp at Epsom, he seemed to be running as one does in a bad dream: the legs move, but they are going nowhere. He finished eighth behind Winged Love (another André Fabre horse) who had taken the race from Definite Article in the very last stride. Third was Annus Mirabilis. He had beaten Celtic Swing by almost as great a distance as he, himself, had lost by in the Racing Post Trophy.

After the race, I realised how strong the hope had still been for Celtic Swing's victory: my certainty that it would not happen had derived, indeed, from my fear of expressing precisely such a hope. If he had won, he would not have been the horse that we had expected him to be, but there would still have been a realistic, robust joy in him. 'Not a great horse,' we would have said, remembering his evasion of Epsom's absolute judgement, 'but bloody good. Brave. Gutsy. A smashing horse.' These were thoughts that I had been longing to have; and that, as the Irish Derby field rounded the turn at The Curragh, I had hoped would be mine.

In the moment that Celtic Swing seemed to stop, his big open stride no longer taking him forwards, the thousands of miles between us did not exist. I forgot the light and lazy afternoon in New York, the idiot announcer and the joke Irishman. I was penetrated by the pain of loss: the certainty, indeed at last the knowledge, that this horse would never do what I had wanted him to do.

There was consolation, of a perverse kind, when I returned to England. Celtic Swing was injured, with damaged knee ligaments, and would not race again in 1995. It is hoped, still, that he will return as a four-year-old: he would still be a more popular horse than any other. There is, still, with him, a sense of unfinished business; perhaps there always will be.

When I learned of his injury, I realised that he had not been himself when he ran in the Irish Derby. How could I have thought, for a moment, that he was? Celtic Swing, who had subjected the turf to his absolute mastery, could not, without reason, have submitted to it so abjectly. Some commentators, who had perceived in the horse a steady and continual decline, were willing to see the Irish Derby result as the inevitable conclusion to this. As they did so, they were flagrantly unfaithful to the memories of 1994; and to the expectations that these had created, and which were now causing Celtic Swing's achievements to be branded as failures.

John Francome, a wiser analyst than these, said in the 1995 Flat Review of the Year video that 'we know now that Celtic Swing was wrong before the Irish Derby . . . I'm sure that he wasn't absolutely right at all last season, and if that was so, he was a really brave racehorse.' This opinion was a comfort because it implied, somehow, that the 1995 races were not the 'real' Celtic Swing: that this magical entity had been betrayed by his external frame, by the nuts and bolts of his growing young body. Of course, this is my interpretation of Francome's words, and one that I know to be overly romantic, but I like to think that the earthly Pegasus was still there, inside the proud and gleaming horse, when he ran the lowlier races of his adult career. It pleased me to believe this; even as the eighth place in the Irish Derby told me, beyond any doubt, that the quest for Celtic Swing's greatness was over.

The time to move on had come. To where, though? To Lammtarra, to Pentire, to Winged Love? Was there, amongst those unexpected achievers in 1995, a horse that could take up the season's broken thread? Or was the quest for greatness over? Had it ended, for this year at least, when Pennekamp defeated Celtic Swing, and then was defeated himself by the unforgiving turf of Epsom? Would 1995 be the opposite of what had been expected: a season, in fact, over which no single horse had true mastery? This thought was hard to countenance, in a year which so much yearned for its hunger for greatness to be sated.

Three weeks after the Irish Derby, the King George VI and Queen Elizabeth Diamond Stakes was to be run at Ascot. This is the most prestigious all-age race in the English season, and in 1995 the three-year-olds would be represented by Lammtarra, Pentire and Winged Love.

On that day, 22 July, the summer reached its height. The silks of the jockeys seemed like absolutes of brightness. The racing season glittered like the head of a fountain, throwing out streams whose source and destination were too dazzling to see in the light. Soon, though, the streams would slow, strengthen, show their direction. The colours of the summer would darken and deepen: the sky would become full and heavy blue; the coats of the bay horses would seem to flood with oil; the chestnuts would burn with fires. And, as they did so, the racing season, too, would reveal its deeper pattern.

VII

THROUGHOUT THE LAST two hundred years or so of flat racing's history, in the time since it became recognisable as the sport of today, there have been jockeys whose individuality has compelled their public. They have been few: perhaps one in every generation. The first was probably Samuel Chifney, who began riding in about 1770. He was, indeed, the first true racehorse jockey. Instead of riding his horses flat out from the start, as many American jockeys still do today, he used tactics and developed a late run, known as the 'Chifney Rush'. He would have recognised this in the way that Walter Swinburn rode Lammtarra to his Derby victory.

Although his career ended when the Jockey Club accused him of pulling one of the Prince of Wales's (later George IV) horses, and he died in a debtors' prison, he had revolutionised his sport. He knew it, too; when he published his autobiography in 1795, it was titled *Genius Genuine*. He was a conceited and not especially likeable man, but he had that instinct for the horse which characterises all the great jockeys. Pulling up a mount after a race should be done, he wrote, 'as if you had a silken rein, as thin as a hair, and you were afraid of breaking it'.

Jockeying was revolutionised again, about a century later. This time the innovation actually came from the USA. Before the late nineteenth century, jockeys had ridden sitting back in the saddle, as if their forty mile per hour racehorse was no different from a hunter; but in 1897 the American Tod Sloan brought to England the practice of riding with very short stirrups. They were much longer, in fact, than they would be today, but they still forced Sloan to crouch around the horse's neck: like, wrote *Vanity Fair,* 'a monkey on a stick'. This riding style has been used ever since. It is said to have originated at rough, country meetings in the USA. Black boys, who had never learned to ride and were given no saddles, simply hung on to the horses' manes and balanced with their lifted knees. When the winning mounts were sold on to better trainers, they were found to have lost their form; the only thing that recaptured it was to bring back the crouching jockeys.

It was, indeed, a black American called Sims who first rode this way in England, where he was laughed off the track. The successes of Tod Sloan, however, forced the style to be taken seriously. Like Chifney, Sloan was unlikeable and immodest; he was also a terrible gambler. One feels a certain sympathy for his rages in the Newmarket weighing room, after losing a winning bet of around £150,000 in the 1900 Cambridgeshire handicap, but they led to him being banned by the Jockey Club from racing in England.

Fred Archer, who had achieved success about ten years before Sloan, was a very different kind of man. He was perhaps the first jockey to achieve true sporting hero status: the phrase 'Archer's Up' (meaning that he was in the saddle) became an English way of saying that things couldn't be better. He had a romantic appearance, unusually tall and with a beautiful, moulded and mournful face. Matthew Dawson, who trained St Simon at Newmarket, paid Archer a retainer to work for him, but before receiving this he had already, at the age of seventeen, become champion jockey. He was to do so twelve times in his career.

By 1886, the year in which he won his fifth and last Derby on Ormonde, he was finding it increasingly hard to make racing weights. He had been too heavy to ride St Simon in his great Gold Cup triumph and now, although he used a purgative of appalling strength and fasted for three days before the 1886 Cambridgeshire, he still put up a pound overweight at eight stone eight, and lost the race by a head.

He shot himself in the mouth only a month afterwards. He was twenty-nine. He was still suffering depression over the death of his wife, two years earlier, but there is little doubt that this was compounded by his continual struggle to achieve a weight two or three stones too low for his body. Fasting had made him ill with typhoid fever, and it had probably made him mad.

The twentieth century has been dominated, so far, by three great jockeys. Steve Donoghue was champion ten times from 1914 to 1922. He rode The Tetrarch, who in 1913 won all his two-year-old races in a disdainful canter, then knocked a fetlock at the end of the season and never raced again; had circumstances been different, Celtic Swing might have been another such horse. Donoghue also rode Brown Jack, perhaps the most popular horse who ever raced on the flat, and his own favourite. Brown Jack was a tractable, kindly gelding, very different from most of his kind, charged as they are with so much nervous, defiant energy. On the day of his sixth Queen Alexandra Stakes at Ascot in 1934, the *Evening Standard* headlines read, simply, 'Brown Jack Today'. His victory must have been one of the greatest sporting occasions of the century. Donoghue wrote of the race that 'all my six Derbies faded before the reception that was awaiting Jack and myself as we set out to return to weigh in. Never will I forget the roar of that crowd as long as I live.'

Sir Gordon Richards's total of 269 winners in the 1947 season has never been beaten. It is an extraordinary record to hold, when one considers that jockeys today have fast cars and planes to take them to meetings, and they can work through the whole year on the winter all-weather tracks. Richards won almost one in four races that he rode. He was champion jockey twenty-six times; although, amazingly, he rode only one Derby winner, Pinza in 1953 (in her Coronation year, the Queen's own runner was second). He retired that season: only four times since then has a champion jockey ridden more than 200 winners.

And then there is Piggott: nine Derbies, five Two Thousand Guineas, two One Thousand Guineas, six Oaks, eight St Legers. Like Fred Archer, Lester Piggott was tall and always striving for a weight two stones below what would be considered natural; as Dick Francis wrote, 'on a clear day you can see right through him.' But Piggott was the greatest jockey of the past forty years, and probably of the century. He was fierce, and fearless, and his race tactics included distracting jockeys who presented a threat to him: rather like John McEnroe playing tennis. His horsemanship, though, was unparalleled. He would seem to be doing nothing, just gliding along with the horse, almost motionless, almost upside-down; but then, mysteriously, the horse would appear in the right position, at the right time, and a sense of inevitability would infuse the race.

Sometimes it would seem easy, as when Nijinsky won the Derby. Sometimes it would look as hard as it really was, as when, two years later, Roberto was pushed and pushed past Rheingold to win by the flicker of an eyelash. Piggott said afterwards that Roberto was lazy and disliked left-hand bends: on ability, he said, the horse should have won the Derby by two lengths. Only Piggott could elicit from Roberto the desire to win a race that, in the final furlong, he had made so difficult for himself. He could find things in a horse that other jockeys could not: he could make the partnership between them a perfect one.

With his strained, crumpled face, his evanescent thinness, his deafness, his taciturnity, he was a figure as remote as the animals he rode. In 1995, the year of his (second) retirement, he received from the BBC a lifetime achievement award at the Sports Personality of the Year ceremony. He baffled Sue Barker, whose grim task it was to interview him. 'Who,' she twinkled, 'is the best horse you've ever ridden – do-you-think?!' No doubt she was hoping to hear the name of Nijinsky, to which she could react with some understanding. But Piggott, after pausing for some seconds and creating a very real sense that he would not answer at all, finally raised his exhausted eyebrows and said: 'Sn-Ive'. Sue twinkled on, bright and uncomprehending. 'Yeah, he was the best. Sn-Ive.' At some point it became clear, through the impenetrable nasal of his speech, that he was saying Sir Ivor, but this was Piggott all over; moved as he obviously was to receive the award, he was not going to give in to pressure and start talking: bandying names, remembering the good old days of Nijinsky and The Minstrel and, ah, in his very first Derby of all, Never Say Die, all those many years ago. Instead he would tell the truth; say the name of a horse that few people in his audience would remember; and say no more.

This is the wonderful thing about jockeys. They do not move in the world of interviews and self-promotion and marketing, whose bright light shines upon everything with the same, lifeless sheen: publicly, indeed, jockeys do not move in the world of human beings. Their understanding, always, is with the horse, something of whose mystique they hold within their starved, tough, little bodies.

Most sports stars are absorbed in solipsism, and in a world in which their every word is swallowed, chewed fifty times, regurgitated and seasoned with significance. It is hard, therefore, for them to avoid banalities, to retain mystique. The world is too much with them. What they do, magnificent as it often is, cannot be left alone: it must be pulled apart, analysed, reduced to nothingness. 'How did you feel when you won?' 'Did you mind losing?' 'Are you glad to have the gold medal round your neck?' And most sports stars, circumscribed as they are by the need for their image to gleam ever brightly on the media horizon, reply dutifully that they feel delighted for the boys, that they are gutted for the boys, that they are thrilled for themselves but owe it all to their coach. It is boring beyond belief, and everyone knows that it is, though there seems now to be no stopping it.

Jockeys, on the other hand, are the interpreters between us and the horse. They do not tell us what we have all just seen, perfectly well, for ourselves; they tell us things that, otherwise, we would simply not know. There is no self-consciousness, no self-proclamation, no embarrassment or fake modesty or platitudes. For they are not talking about *themselves*; they are talking about themselves *in relationship to the horse*; and, as they do so, they seem almost to be working out the mysteries of this relationship for themselves. The race is still, in a way, going on. Why did the horse do that? Why didn't it do what we expected? What will it do next time? The jockeys are coming, as nearly as possible, to explaining the inexplicable – the mysteries of the racehorse – and then, as always, they stop short. '*I* don't know!' shouted Willie Carson at Julian Wilson, on BBC1, when asked if Bahri would stay a mile and a quarter. 'We've got to wait and find out!' In a world where people will say anything rather than that, it was a fascinating admission.

The jockey's mind is, indeed, a precious thing, for it moves within a world that we cannot see. And, because it is in that world, it has a freshness, an honesty, an individuality; it does not deal in the communal deck of cliché. Even when the jockey says almost nothing, like Piggott, he does at least mean the things that he says. Even as the jockey is talking about the horse – what the horse did, what the horse felt – he is drawing, with indirect but clear strokes, the lines of his own personality.

By comparison with most sports stars, jockeys seem unusually sharp and quick, as if their minds, like their bodies, are close to the bone. Carson is one of the most delicious interviewees imaginable: like a furious bird he stares into the eyes of his questioner, waiting for a mistake or an idiocy, then pounces as if upon a worm. He cannot but express absolutely what is in his mind. When, in 1988, the Queen inexplicably removed her horses from Major Dick

Hern, and her racing manager, Lord Carnarvon, forced the wheel-chair-bound trainer to leave his yard, Carson, as Hern's retained jockey, was unafraid to speak out in condemnation. The following year, Nashwan won the Derby; and the triumphant shake of the fist that Carson gave to Hern, as they met in the winners' enclosure, was more eloquent than any of his protests. 'We fucking showed them,' was what it said.

Because jockeys inhabit a remote world, and most other sports stars have never been more accessible, their racing achievements receive little of the attention given to footballers, rugby players or athletes. These are the people who are described as brave, and dedicated, and determined; accolades are heaped upon them until they tower like heroes.

Yet what they do bears no comparison with the lives of jockeys. Jockeys really *are* brave: they risk injury, even death, with every ride as they grapple with their huge, highly-strung, often recalcitrant mounts, powering round bends and down hills at forty miles an hour, another horse six inches away from them, or trying to pass them, or lurching into them, or going for the gap that should have been theirs.

They really are dedicated: up at ridiculous hours to go on the gallops, driving and flying between meetings every afternoon and evening. The less successful ones amongst them must search all the time for rides. When they are truly successful, they might race over one thousand times in a year (Frankie Dettori had 1,319 rides in his 1994 championship season, of which he won 233).

And they really are determined: sweating off weight every day in saunas, unable ever to relax and rest and eat. Anyone who has ever dieted will know how difficult it can make the rest of your life. Energy and sleep become elusive, the cold becomes vicious, headaches are almost constant; there is a sense of being ever on the alert, of never being allowed to drop the guard against natural impulses. This is how jockeys live all the time. It is easier for some than others, of course: Fred Archer was 5ft 8½ in at a time when jockeys were expected to make even lower weights than today, whereas a man like Carson is so small that it is almost normal for him to be racing weight. But when people talk about the magnificent toughness of rugby players, for example, rolling around a pitch or pushing against each other in scrums, then I think about what they have eaten for breakfast and laugh. Wrestling with 250 pounds of tighthead prop, when your body is practically made of carbohydrate, is one thing. Wrestling with 1,000 pounds of thoroughbred horse, when all that is inside you is a Ryvita and a puff of cigar smoke, is another entirely.

Over the last twenty years several fine jockeys have emerged into the racing world, though not quite from Lester Piggott's spindle shadow. Carson of course; Pat Eddery, with his consistently immaculate timing and, in the 1980s, his four superb wins in the Prix de l'Arc de Triomphe; the American Steve Cauthen, who won the 1985 Derby with a fearless audacity, taking Slip Anchor to the front before the horse had even rounded Tattenham Corner; Walter Swinburn, who, with Shergar, Shahrastani and Lammtarra, won three Derbies which were, in their completely different ways, among the most spectacular of recent years.

And, since 1987, there has been Lanfranco – Frankie – Dettori. He won eight races in that first season. In 1994 and 1995 he was champion jockey. He is also, beyond doubt, the most compelling jockey of a generation; and, in my opinion, the most compelling sportsman.

Like all jockeys, he expresses his personality clearly, freshly and honestly. Unlike some of them, he has a personality that cannot help but delight and entrance. His energy is absolute: whether he is riding, or speaking, or celebrating, whatever he is doing, he gives to it his whole self, a completeness of attention and vitality.

The most irresistible thing about him is his voice. Born in Milan in 1970, the son – as is so often the case – of a jockey, Gianfranco, he joined trainer Luca Cumani as an apprentice in Newmarket at the age of fifteen. His accent seems, though, to be a mixture of Italian and Cockney. The two battle against each other – the one trying to lilt, the other striving for glottal stops – as Dettori races through every sentence at speed, pausing occasionally for exclamation marks, employing phrases of peculiarly English idiom. '*E went-a pasta me loike Oi was a-standing-a steel* – !' was one comment, after Walter Swinburn, on Lammtarra, had overtaken Tamure in the final yards of the Derby.

In the 1994 season he became truly established in the racing world. He had acquired a retainer to ride the Sheikh Mohammed-owned horses in John Gosden's yard, which helped immeasurably in making him champion jockey (although the title was secured by his willingness to ride through the winter on the all-weather tracks; as of 1996, these meetings no longer count towards the championship). He won his first classics, on Balanchine, in the Oaks and Irish Derby; and achieved a remarkable success on Barathea in the Breeders' Cup Mile in the USA. What drew him to public attention, however, even more than these great triumphs, was his riding of the sprint mare Lochsong.

Dettori had ridden her before, in 1993, when she was already five years old, but her owner, Jeff Smith, decided not to retire her, as she was simply getting better and better. She was, in fact, almost a freak. When she galloped at the Breeders' Cup track in Kentucky, two days before her run in the Sprint, she covered the final three furlongs in 33.1 seconds; those who watched her believed that their watches must have broken. As she sometimes did, she had exhausted herself for the race itself, in which she ran last. But during the 1994 season she had, ridden by Dettori, won the King's Stand Stakes at Royal Ascot, the King George Stakes at Goodwood and, most magnificently of all, her second Prix de l'Abbaye at Longchamp, a sprint race run before the Prix de l'Arc de Triomphe. I was there, and remember the way in which she won: from the front, full of awareness, a great mare controlling the field with her breathtaking, voracious speed. I remember the shout of 'Monster!' as Dettori leaped from her back: such was his sense of her power. I remember, too, the kiss that he gave afterwards to her soft horse mouth. He did for me then what I wanted to do myself; and I knew that this was a man with whom I could share the pleasure of victory.

With his effervescence, his leaps from the saddle, his kisses, his smiles that possess the whole of his face, Dettori gives us the sense that he is more accessible than any other jockey. In a way, he is. His reactions are so clearly ours as well. In a remote sport, he is a means of getting closer. He is, as they say, the housewives' choice, the jockey upon whom people who know little about racing can always have a gamble. He is 'Frankie': in the stands, in the betting shops, in the commentaries.

There is, though, an elusiveness about him. I felt it strongly when I met him. It was not that he was holding back at all: he talked wonderfully, and at length, even though he was about to go and ride (on the Lingfield all-weather). His exuberance had that rare and delicious ability to make me feel exuberant also; his charm was compelling. He was the sports star whom I had most wanted to meet, and he was all that I had hoped he would be.

But he is, too, a great talent, dealing in a world that only he and his kind understands, and this gives him an essential impenetrability. For all his generosity with his energy, he is self-possessed, self-contained. What he shows his public is not an act; it is the real man, but it is also a display, almost a deflection, from the mysterious and undistracted centre. In this, Frankie Dettori is like all jockeys: like the horses that he rides.

In 1995, Dettori had, by the mid-summer, ridden his second Oaks winner with Moonshell, and had also ridden Vettori to victory in the French Two Thousand Guineas. He had been within yards of winning the Derby, on Tamure, when Lammtarra passed him.

'It took me a while to get by the leader, Fahal, and I just got by in the last hundred yards. And I thought then, for arf a second – this is it, we've done it. No longer than arf a second. And then all of a sudden Lammtarra came by. I must say (*Oi mast-a say-a*), it was a very fast run race, and we weren't exactly sprinting, you know. I wasn't really finishing, I was running on one pace. And, like, Lammtarra just found his feet, and he just – flew! – past us. And, I must say, I'm glad he beat me a length – ! – not a short head. But, I must say, he's paid me back since then.'

This last sentence refers to the fact that, on 19 July, three days before the King George VI and Queen Elizabeth Diamond Stakes was to be run at Ascot, it was announced that Frankie Dettori would take over the ride on Lammtarra from Walter Swinburn.

This news met with astonishment, and some disgust, in the racing world. After Swinburn had ridden Lammtarra so magnificently in the Derby, and had galloped him in all his preparatory work at Newmarket, it seemed incomprehensible that he should lose the ride. Dettori is a tremendous jockey, but there has never been any suggestion that he was better than Swinburn: only opinion could give preference to one or the other. However, Simon Crisford, the racing manager for Godolphin, said that 'Frankie Dettori is the stable jockey and it has been decided that he will ride Lammtarra.' In other words, Dettori had the ride because he was Sheikh Mohammed's retained jockey.

This was an argument, of sorts, though not a very good one: as one newspaper put it at the time, Crisford had been left to 'defend the indefensible'. Swinburn rode plenty of Godolphin horses; they could not all be given to Dettori. The suspicion was that Dettori had been given the ride for other reasons, though these were never confirmed. There was, for example, a suggestion that Swinburn had angered Sheikh Mohammed by failing to ride two of the Al Maktoum family's horses in Paris the week before, and failing to provide a good enough excuse for his absence. It certainly seemed that there was something punitive about the decision to jock off Swinburn. When questioned about it, Sheikh Mohammed warned journalists not to 'fish in shallow waters', as if there were some reason behind his decision that it was best not to expose. But the feeling persisted that Swinburn had been treated badly, and gave some people an excuse, for which they had perhaps longed, to vent their buried resentment of the Al Maktoums. They are, no doubt, autocratic men; what they did to Swinburn showed as much. Yet it would be hard to think of them as dishonourable. Whatever the reason for giving Lammtarra to Dettori, it would, in the mind of Sheikh Mohammed at least, have been a proper and a principled one.

In its different ways, though, it must have been very difficult for the two jockeys. Without ever directly commenting on what had happened, each man conveyed something of this discomfort and of the friendship that survived it. Dettori: 'I don't know really what happened, politics-wise, but let's not get into that. Wally helped me a lot before the race. He said to me, Frankie, dig deep with Lammtarra, because he will keep finding more for you.'

'Frankie was kind enough,' says Swinburn, who sounded remarkably calm and free of bitterness, 'after the King George, to say that I gave him some help.'

It was not an unprecedented occurrence. Jockeys do lose rides; when Lester Piggott was working as a freelance, unattached to any stable, there was always a danger that an owner would claim him for a big race ride. It happened, of course, with Roberto. It happened to Walter Swinburn's father, when he lost to Piggott the ride on Blue Wind, who won the Oaks in 1981. This was a little different, though, as Swinburn senior had in fact agreed to this switch; it was certainly a more amicable arrangement than that which was forced upon his son, fourteen years later.

It tainted the build-up to a race that was already being regarded with subdued interest. There seemed, even, to be some sulking going on: who, after all, was this damn Lammtarra? Was he really to be favourite for the King George VI and Queen Elizabeth Diamond Stakes, a race that had been won by Ribot, Nijinsky and Mill Reef, by Brigadier Gerard, The Minstrel and Shergar, by Dancing Brave, Nashwan and Generous? Was he really the best that the 1995 season could come up with: this unknown horse with his two runs, his forgotten two-year-old race and his freakish Derby?

And what of the rest? Pentire, a horse who had not even contested a classic race. Winged Love, winner of an Irish Derby that had caused even more sulking (who, after all, was Winged Love?). Then the older horses: Carnegie, who had won the 1994 Arc but done little since. Broadway Flyer, second in the 1994 St Leger. Environment Friend, the game old grey, who had been a fine member of the 1991 classic fields but was now seven years of age. Strategic Choice, whose last win had been a Group Three race.

This was one way of looking at it; another was to see three classic winners, three former classic contenders and, in Pentire, a horse of clear classic potential. Pentire was, indeed, the 6–4 ante-post favourite, with Lammtarra and Carnegie both at 11–4.

This proved what had already been hinted: observers believed that the 'Derby form' was suspect, and that Lammtarra had looked, in that race, a great deal better than he was. Court of Honour, Munwar and Humbel had finished further behind Winged Love in the Irish Derby than they had behind Lammtarra at Epsom. Presenting, Fahal and Vettori had all lost their races subsequent to the Derby. What, then, had Lammtarra flown past, in those final furlongs?

This 'Derby form' business is always an obsession, and always an irritant. Horses, as is constantly proved, hardly ever run the same race twice; they are vulnerable to an almost infinite number of variables, including ground, distance, race tactics, fluctuations in their well-being. They can also take longer than is always realised to recover from a hard race like the Derby. They look right, they move right, but they don't necessarily feel right. When Nijinsky won the St Leger in 1970, he had suffered, for some time before the race, with a ring worm fungus which had affected his preparation and his health. On the day of the Leger, he looked perfect and, although the mile and three-quarters was a little too far for him, he won the race by a length. Afterwards, he was found to have lost twenty-nine pounds. He ran twice more in his career, but he never won again.

This is Nijinsky: the great Nijinsky, proving the susceptibility of these magnificent but fragile animals, and the impossibility of knowing quite what is going on inside their bodies. Perhaps there were good reasons why the Derby field did not win its subsequent races. Perhaps, even if they had won, it would have been said that they, in their turn, were not beating much. The middle of a season is hardly the time to pronounce definitively on their abilities.

Notwithstanding the doubts about the 'Derby form', *The Times* wrote of the King George that 'a victory for either Lammtarra or Pentire would rekindle from the dying embers the dreams of greatness. It will be their opportunity to pick up the baton from Celtic Swing and Pennekamp.'

The King George VI and Queen Elizabeth Diamond Stakes has a short history. It was named, on its inauguration in 1951, in honour of the present Queen's parents, and acquired the 'diamond' in its title in 1975, to acknowledge its sponsorship by de Beers. In the past it has been the richest race of the season though, due to Vodafone's sponsorship of the Derby, this was not the case in 1995: the winning prize money was £278,760, compared with the Derby's £504,500.

As an all-aged contest the King George does not have, perhaps, the resonance of the Prix de l'Arc de Triomphe; yet it could be said that the Ascot race provides the truest of all tests for the thorough-bred. Every horse can run in it, and every horse has a fair chance.

Longchamp is a magnificent course, but its races are often affected by the draw from the stalls, which can leave horses on the outside at a strong disadvantage. The draw for Ascot's mile and a half is generally less vital; the course undulates, though to nothing like the extent of Epsom. It forms a smooth triangle, which the horses travel clockwise, whose only real difficulty is presented by the unusually short finishing straight. A race such as Lammtarra ran in the Derby, when he made up so much ground after rounding Tattenham Corner, would be impossible at Ascot.

As was the case in 1995, the fields for the King George have often been small. Surprisingly, considering that a horse develops in strength between the ages of three and four, the race has been won by 25 three-year-olds, compared with 16 four-year-olds and only 4 five-year-olds. Five fillies have won, one of them twice; and, including Lammtarra, the race has been won by fourteen Epsom Derby winners.

In its forty-five runnings are contained some of the greatest races of recent years: the King George has honoured its victors and, almost always, shown them at their best. Compared with the Derby's huge fields and rumbustious running, the King George has a look of simplicity, as if the season has pared itself down to essentials. This is not necessarily the case; but the race never seems, as others so often do, to be carrying superfluous runners. For example, when Nijinsky won in 1970, he beat the winners of two Derbies, the French Oaks, the Coronation Cup (run at Epsom) and the Washington International (run in the USA). This was an outstanding field, even by King George standards, but Nijinsky won the race in a canter – it was the easiest victory of his career. 'He's trotted up!' says Peter O'Sullevan on the commentary, almost laughing with delight. 'What a horse this is.'

After Nijinsky, the two other great horses of the 1970s

triumphed in the race. Mill Reef's was a magnificent, six-length victory; Brigadier Gerard's was his fifteenth consecutive win, in which he bravely stayed on half a mile further than the distance at which he was truly supreme.

In the next two years, the race was won by the same horse, the filly Dahlia. As a three-year-old, she too achieved a six-length victory in which she beat the 1972 Derby first and second, Roberto and Rheingold. She was owned by an American, Nelson Bunker Hunt, and eventually retired to his stud farm. However, after the crash in the USA breeding market, caused by the end of the auction battles between Robert Sangster and the Al Maktoums, Bunker Hunt was forced to sell his farm and his horses. Dahlia, by this time, was eighteen years old.

In his wonderful book, *Horsetrader*, which tells the story of Sangster and the American breeders, Patrick Robinson describes the sale of Dahlia at the Keeneland auctions. He writes of how a respectful hush pervaded the ring when she was led in, the memories of her triumphs filling the minds of all present, and of the quiet sigh of relief when she was sold to Allen Paulson, the owner of a beautiful American stud farm. That day, Keeneland received an anonymous telephone call, inquiring who had bought the mare. The caller was Nelson Bunker Hunt: in the midst of his financial ruin, his only thought then was to know that Dahlia was safe.

Perhaps the greatest of the King Georges – the greatest of races, according to some – was its 1975 running. The final furlong saw a fight, to the line, between Bustino and the Derby winner, Grundy. Bustino had the lead from three furlongs out; then Grundy wrenched it away from him; then Bustino fought back; and throughout the final furlong the two horses ran side by side, ears flat against the wind, veins and bones pushing against the smooth shape of their heads, until, on the line, Grundy gave a last effort that beat off Bustino. Their desperate struggle for supremacy caused the race to be run almost two and a half seconds faster than it had ever yet been. It finished the careers of both horses: Bustino never ran again, and Grundy only once, finishing fourth.

The nobility of racehorses is such that they do not naturally arouse feelings of pity: to watch them is always moving, but only touching when they reveal vulnerability. The 1975 King George was such a time. Despite the fact that Bustino and Grundy were displaying all the nobility of which their breed is capable, their unquestioning willingness to commit every inch of body, every ounce of heart, showed what they will give for the sport that we love, and that they serve. It was a great, great race; but it was a little too much. It left within its awesome, glittering memory a faint shadow of sadness, even of shame.

The final furlong of the 1995 King George VI and Queen Elizabeth Diamond Stakes was the nearest thing to the Bustino-Grundy fight to have been seen in the race for twenty years, although it did not quite convey that same quality of desperation. As the press and the bookmakers had predicted, Lammtarra and Pentire battled to the line for victory, and for the claim to be considered the best of the season.

Frankie Dettori: 'When I go to ride Lammtarra at Ascot, I only had three days before the race. I never really actually sat on him, but I saw him many times. I rode a few pacemakers and Wally rode Lammtarra. And I thought, well, from what I know about the horse (*thee oarse-a*) – I thought, well, the horse is very tough, stays the distance good, and he's only run twice, you know? So I can't afford to play too much jockeying – ! Because Ascot, the run-in is less than Epsom.

'So. I think I'm on the best horse. I was drawn on the outside, and I thought, I don't mind losing a bit of ground on the turns. At least I can keep the horse smooth, and I can go whenever I feel like it. That was my plan.

'And then, when we got to the start, Lammtarra – well, you

144

know, he's different. He's not very straightforward. He's not a horse what is normal. He has his moments, you know – ! And he started to whip round, he didn't want to go . . . But obviously, before a big race like that you don't force a horse to do what you want. You try and veer and go with him. He's been like that in the mornings, anyhow, so it was nothing unusual. But in that moment, when you're trying to concentrate on something and he's not being helpful . . . It was a little bit difficult.'

This show of temperament from Lammtarra made me think of Ezzoud. It was a year since I had watched him prancing behind the stalls, jerking his masked head and planning his coup. The 1994 running had been the worst King George in the history of the race, a travesty when compared with the great and noble victories of the 1970s. It was, nonetheless, the most compelling and significant race that I had ever seen; because of it, I knew more than I would once have thought possible about the horses in the 1995 King George.

I had seen Carnegie triumph in the Arc, and Winged Love gallop away from Celtic Swing in the Irish Derby. I had seen Pentire's decisive surge at Royal Ascot, and Lammtarra's strange and spectacular flight down the straight at Epsom, which now seemed almost to have happened in a dream. I was not, as I had been a year ago, electrified by the tiny connections that I could make between Ezzoud and Erhaab, breathless with the new sensation of recognition. The 1994 race had come at me like an assault: by the end of it, the emotions it had aroused of delight and excitement, fear and love were standing inside me like a hedgehog's spikes. Now, a year later and still stunned by the events that had led up to the King George, I was unsure what to make of it. I had had no bet in the race, which was unusual for me; this seemed to prove that I was, simply, waiting to see what would happen.

For a long time, indeed for about a mile, the answer to that was: nothing. Broadway Flyer led, as he almost always did, from the first. Behind him, the field was bunched contentedly, Lammtarra and

Pentire towards the rear. As was to be expected in such a small field, it looked as though every horse, except the leader, was carefully biding its time.

Halfway through the race, around seven lengths separated the seven horses: Broadway Flyer was at the front, Pentire at the back. Lammtarra ran on the outside of Carnegie, his power concealed behind the shield of his impassivity. As the race approached the final turn, he looked to me the most likely winner. Watching him, poised as he seemed to be with such exquisite imminence, I felt within me the fluttering rush of his Derby victory. Suddenly, it became a reality again: surely, I thought, the horse who had passed through that field with such supremacy, such indifference, could take possession of this King George at any moment?

Dettori: 'I thought, well, after we pass the four furlongs, I might get a little bit close. But, as I asked him, he didn't respond like I thought he would. I was at him – I had to ask him a little bit. I gave him arf a furlong to find his feet and still . . . he was coming on, but he wasn't coming on like I expected – !'

Lammtarra had not, indeed, made a move forward. My ignorance, at that time, of the short home straight at Ascot led me to believe that this was not yet necessary: that he could win the race as he had the Derby. The horses rounded the first bend of the final turn. Strategic Choice began to advance on Broadway Flyer; Pentire moved up on Lammtarra; Carnegie and Winged Love, both in Sheikh Mohammed's colours, were cut off on the inside. Then, as the horses turned the corner of the bend, Environment Friend swung out and gave Lammtarra a slight push.

'It made me go wide – but perhaps it helped him, you know? It woke him up. He thought: Ah – ! – it's time to run.'

Turning into the home straight, the race became possessed, at last, by a sense of shape and urgency. As one, the three horses on the outside – Environment Friend, Lammtarra and Pentire – swooped upon the lead. Then Environment Friend seemed to check, moving suddenly to the back of the field, where Carnegie still lingered; at the front, they were running in a line of four: Broadway Flyer, Strategic Choice, Lammtarra, Pentire. From this position, I felt sure that at any moment Lammtarra would simply leap away from them. Two furlongs out, however, Pentire took the lead.

'All of a sudden, Pentire looms upsides me on the bridle. *But.* The way we were quickening, give another furlong, and I knew I was going to get Lammtarra off the bridle.'

It looked like a battle. Lammtarra looked to be fighting, as Grundy had done, to beat off this indomitable challenge: not just from Pentire but from Strategic Choice, who was running the race of his life. The horses – three of them now – were still moving in a line. However, at some point inside the final furlong, there was a quick, almost unnoticeable push from Lammtarra to which there was no possible response. Suddenly, his lean bright body had the lead: it was stretched long and low, like an old-style painting of a racehorse, while, on his outside, Pentire's stride grew shorter and shorter. The battle continued to the line. Lammtarra won the race by only a neck. Yet somewhere in those last few seconds he had made it certain that he would do so.

There were observers who said that Pentire had come for the lead too soon: like Celtic Swing in the Two Thousand Guineas, he had lost the race by putting himself in a position where Lammtarra could attack him. This may be the case. It cannot be proved. It did not, somehow, look that way; nor does Dettori describe it that way. For all the narrowness of his victory, Lammtarra seemed to have the absolute measure of the race. Unlike Grundy, he seemed still to be within himself. It was as different a win as could be conceived from that of the Derby: here was no glamorous sweep through the field, no sense that Lammtarra had become speed incarnate. Yet, in some mysterious way, the two races still gave the same impression: of a horse running a race of his own. In essence, Lammtarra had

147

done at Ascot what he had done before, at Epsom and at Newbury. He had, as Swinburn said he would, done exactly what was necessary: no more, no less.

Dettori: 'Not winning by much – that's just im. Just im. He enjoyed racing, and he liked it like that. I think, even if you dropped him down in class, he would win by the same margin. He liked the challenge, he liked the fight. It's weird, you know.

'A million years ago, OK, horses were in this world, and the only way to get away from predators was to run. So horses run with fear. Especially fillies, what are very delicate. They have no purpose, they don't know they're passing the winning post, they run until you tell them to stop. But Lammtarra – no. He wasn't one of those. You had to make him run. And he had a purpose. He didn't run for the sake of it – he liked to run and win by a length, because he enjoyed being in the race.

'I think he *really* enjoyed it. He enjoyed being in the nitty-gritty of things, making life really difficult for everybody. I think he *loved* that.'

It is strange to go from Frankie Dettori's delighted relish in this horse, his admiration for the independent spirit which grew, in rhythm, with the increase in power and experience, to the joyless reception for Lammtarra's victory in the King George VI and Queen Elizabeth Diamond Stakes. All right – it seemed to say – he had proved that the Derby win was not, exactly, a fluke; but to win by a neck, with Pentire, Strategic Choice, Winged Love and Broadway Flyer so close behind – well, it just was not good enough. The expected contest between Lammtarra and Pentire had materialised. Somehow, though, it had not quite proved what it was meant to prove.

Although my feelings are now very different, at the time I understood this reaction. Beforehand, I had not quite known what to make of the race. Afterwards, I felt the same way – and it was

Lammtarra who was baffling me. I understood so little then of a horse's nature, of the infinite depths of mystery that lay within it. I did not know that a horse might, in a sense, *choose* the way in which it won a race.

Halfway through the King George, I had expected Lammtarra's victory. The memory of his Derby had flashed through me – that blind rush, that impossible acceleration – and, with it, had come the desire to feel again the vast emotions that it had aroused. Here, I thought, beginning to fill with anticipation, is the horse who will loosen these accumulations of hope. Here is the one who will take up the quest for greatness. Like the triumphal leader of a tired army, Lammtarra will run towards the sun, his chestnut body gleaming and his colours washed clear by the brightness. This is what, for a few brief moments, I thought would happen. Yet, although victory came, it did not do so in that way. Rigorous as always, flat racing took from me my expectations and gave me the reality instead. It gave me Lammtarra, who did things in his own way, who was elusive and impenetrable, who was a beat ahead of those who watched him; I, for one, on the day of the King George, had not yet caught up with him.

VIII

THERE WERE TEN WEEKS between the 1995 King George VI and Queen Elizabeth Diamond Stakes and the Prix de l'Arc de Triomphe. During that time, as in the comparable period before the Derby, Lammtarra retreated into invisibility. There was talk, at first, that he would run a preparatory race for the Arc; in the subsequent silence, it became clear that this was not the way in which Lammtarra did things.

There was never any suggestion that he would contest the St Leger, though it used to be that horses who had won the Derby would, unless they were clearly incapable of running a mile and three-quarters, automatically run the race. Despite the fact that it still forms the third leg of racing's Triple Crown, the St Leger has declined in status over the last twenty years or so. This is not – as is the case with the Derby – because fewer people attend the meeting, but because fewer good horses contest the race.

Partly this is connected to the growing obsession with breeding unduly fast horses, who will then, it is hoped, stay a mile and a half. It is also to do with the fact that the St Leger comes only three weeks or so before the Prix de l'Arc de Triomphe. There are several theories as to why Nijinsky failed, by a neck, to win the Arc, but it seems almost certain that he would have won had he not run in the Leger; since then, the race has failed to attract the great horses that it once did. A year later, in 1971, Mill Reef went straight from the King George to the Arc. Lammtarra was to do the same thing.

In his absence, the ante-post favourite for the St Leger was Presenting, who had run third behind Lammtarra at Epsom. Presenting had lost his first race after the Derby but, three days after the King George, he triumphed decisively in the Gordon Stakes on the first day of the 'Glorious' Goodwood meeting. Goodwood is the most relaxed of all the big meetings, and disseminates the kindliest, least frenetic atmosphere. This may be to do with its setting on top of the Sussex Downs, whose smooth unchanging aspect reminds the spectator that this sport is, after all, about the natural magnificence of horses running across countryside. It seemed fitting, therefore, that this was the meeting to remind us that the 'Derby form' is something to be admired and respected, not picked at and examined for holes. Presenting lifted his fine brown head and scented the mood. His handsome, regular action skated lovingly across the hard ground to set a new course record; as he crossed the winning line, the Derby form seemed suddenly very different.

Shortly afterwards, he won the Group Two Geoffrey Freer Stakes at Newbury. He loved the extra furlong, he loved the sun-baked turf. The only thing that could stop him from winning the St Leger, it seemed, was rain.

After Goodwood came the big meeting at York, in which, on 15 August, Pentire contested the Great Voltigeur Stakes. He won by the shortest of heads, in a finish far closer than that of the King George. This could have been interpreted as a knock back to the boost that Presenting had given to Lammtarra's form; conversely, it revealed as clearly as possible Pentire's fighting qualities. This was especially true as the horse was thought to look somewhat dispirited in the close, stifling circle of the paddock. It may well have been that giving all, against Lammtarra, was an experience from which it took more than three and a half weeks to recover.

Second to Pentire at York was Singspiel who had – it now

seemed a very long time ago – finished eight lengths behind Celtic Swing at Ascot. He had also run second in the Coral-Eclipse Stakes, at Sandown, to a four-year-old named Halling. A Godolphin horse, Halling had won the 1994 Cambridgeshire handicap before wintering in Dubai. Now he too ran at York on 15 August, in the Juddmonte International Stakes. The field included Bahri, Annus Mirabilis and Eltish. It was a good field; but none of them had any chance whatever.

I backed Halling in the race, which was run on one of the hottest days of the summer. I can still feel the sun streaming almost painfully through my window; it fell upon the screen image of the horse as he went to the front two furlongs out, and blinded me with its dazzle as he cantered to the line. He had won the two all-age Group One races that Ezzoud had won the year before. He may not have been so eccentric in his running, but he carried within him an even greater capacity to surprise.

'Horse of the century!' said Willie Carson, who had been left lengths behind on Bahri. It was, indeed, a staggering performance; but what Carson really referred to was the fact that Halling, the year before, had been no more than a handicap horse. He had even finished sixth in a maiden race at Windsor. His victory in the Cambridgeshire showed much improvement; nevertheless, to move from a handicap win to leaving horses like Bahri for dead is, in human terms, like winning an AAA 100 metres and then, the next season, beating Linford Christie to Olympic gold.

Was this, perhaps, a miracle wrought by the Dubai sun? Obviously, Halling had thrived during the winter; but no one, not even Sheikh Mohammed, can put into a horse what is not there. Halling had simply reached his peak at four, rather than at three. He was the finest four-year-old of the 1995 season; but four-year-old greatness is, somehow, a different thing from three-year-old greatness. It is not so absolute. A four-year-old's races may have more weight and grandeur; but they do not bring with them that magnetic, irresistible sense of watching a horse learn, and unfold, and discover, and fulfil, as it measures itself against the classics. Even Halling, for all his wonderful unexpectedness, could not quite convey that. It is arbitrary, of course; in the same way that it is arbitrary to decree that what a horse does at two is only a presage of what it will do at three. But, with the classic races, the flat season has made the three-year-old horse its central figure. What happens before, and what happens next, are always in the nature of a tantalising prologue and a glorious aftermath.

Rain came to Doncaster and Presenting, whose hooves bounced happily off unforgiving ground but sank miserably into the soft, was withdrawn from the St Leger. The race was won easily by the new favourite, Godolphin's Classic Cliché. He gave Frankie Dettori his 1,000th win in Britain; and gave to the Al Maktoums the fifth and final classic of 1995.

At the St Leger meeting, the Laurent-Perrier Champagne Stakes – run over seven furlongs for two-year-olds – was won by the favourite, Alhaarth. Like Pennekamp the year before, he was also to win the Dewhurst Stakes at Newmarket. Like Celtic Swing, he was made favourite for the Two Thousand Guineas and the Derby. He did not run away from the field as Celtic Swing had done; there was no 'Alhaarth first - the rest nowhere'; but he looked, as Celtic Swing had never quite done, like a real racer. I could almost feel the pull within myself, and the racing world, as we tried to resist the desire to see potential greatness in Alhaarth, and, at the same time, searched for it in every inch of him.

This was true, too, of the pair of two-year-old fillies that stretched clear of the rest during 1995. Blue Duster, who had won at Royal Ascot, accelerated to a smooth victory in the Cheveley Park Stakes at Newmarket. Bosra Sham won the Fillies' Mile at Ascot: at 530,000 guineas, she had been the most expensive yearling sold in Europe in 1994, and she pretty well looked it. Her win took place within Ascot's September 'Festival of Racing' meeting, which also contained one of the most extraordinary performances of the season.

The Queen Elizabeth II Stakes, a Group One mile race which was run on 23 September, was expected to be won by Ridgewood Pearl. She was odds-on favourite, with Bahri at 5–2. However, the Irish contingent, who had come to see their big, brave, beloved filly triumph again at Ascot, had reckoned without the cunning of Willie Carson.

'I had to get an edge somehow,' he said after the race, ' because on my book I could not beat the filly on straightforward form.' He knew that the ground would be faster where the track had not been watered; and so, while the rest of the field pursued the mile course close to the rail, Carson took his horse out wide – not just by a few feet, but by yards and yards – and ran beneath the trees. It could have been a disaster, though the fear of that would not have stopped Carson. In fact, by the time he cut across back to the field, he had given Bahri a clear lead.

I have said that a jockey should not, through tactics, win a race with a horse that is not good enough to do so; but this was so auda-cious, so funny, so absolutely the sort of thing that Willie Carson would dare to do *and* would get away with that I could not help but delight in it. I also felt that Bahri would probably have won anyway. Ridgewood Pearl ran a tired race compared with her triumph at Royal Ascot; and Bahri had, after all, been proved a fine miler by his own Royal Ascot win, and his third in both the English and Irish Two Thousand Guineas. He was a couple of lengths clear of Ridgewood Pearl when, three furlongs out, he cut back to the rail. However, he won the race by six lengths.

I was glad, for I had a great fondness for Bahri. He reminded me of a horse called Grand Lodge, who also won the St James's Palace Stakes, and whom I had grown to know during the 1994 season. Both horses raced constantly, always amongst fields of the highest class; in lesser company, they would have triumphed every time. As it was, they were more often competitors than winners, but they ran every race striving for victory. They were emblems of honesty, emblems of effort: to me, they were the rocks upon which the season depended. They could never define greatness, as Celtic Swing and Lammtarra had the potential to do. Instead, they did something smaller but still very precious: they defined a season.

Another boost was given to the Derby form on the day of Bahri's race through the trees, when Riyadian, who had run seventh behind Lammtarra, won the Cumberland Lodge Stakes. A week before this, Tamure, second in the Derby, had won his first subsequent race in the Prix du Prince d'Orange at Longchamp. Spectrum, also racing for the first time since Epsom, was a neck behind him. A couple of weeks later, Court of Honour, fifth in the Derby, won the Group One Gran Premio del Jockey e Coppa d'Oro in Italy.

Strategic Choice, who had run a close third in the King George VI and Queen Elizabeth Diamond Stakes, won the Irish St Leger. He beat the magnificent Vintage Crop, who had won the race in the two previous years, and the Godolphin horse Moonax, who had won the English Leger in 1994. Also in Ireland, Pentire ran his last race of the season when he won the Group One Champion Stakes. In yet another of his devilishly close finishes, and with the most perfectly-timed surge of his career, he beat André Fabre's Freedom Cry by inches.

Lammtarra had retreated from the arena; but, all around him, as he made his invisible preparation for the Prix de l'Arc de Triomphe, the horses that he had beaten were winning, again and again. The true pattern of the season was, it seemed, being drawn with ever deeper and clearer lines. Its central question, though, was still unanswered. Would the threads of the pattern draw themselves to-gether, and bring an end to the quest for greatness? Or would the quest have to wait for a new season: for Alhaarth, perhaps, or for some other two-year-old, or even for some unknown, unnamed yearling?

By the end of September, the sensual heat of the summer had gone, and the fountain of the racing season flowed with a fuller, stronger, more purposeful stream. In Newmarket, the sun no longer fell upon him in the way to which he had become accustomed, but Lammtarra was galloping across the Heath like a fiend, preparing to resolve the pattern.

Of the three-year-old colts who had contested the classic races of 1995, Lammtarra was the only one who would go to the Prix de l'Arc de Triomphe. With him, instead, were Strategic Choice, who had run so well in his last two races; Pure Grain, a gorgeous filly who had had brilliant wins in the Yorkshire and Irish Oaks, and who travelled to the race with her companion horse, in a box lined with mirrors; Luso, who was to be Lammtarra's pacemaker; and Balanchine. She had had the narrowest of defeats against Carnegie, the 1994 Arc winner, at Longchamp in September, and it was believed that she might be returning to her magnificent best.

As well as the German champion, Lando, who had run in the 1994 Arc, the English horses would meet, in France, the strongest of home sides. Carnegie was running again. There were two fine four-year-olds: Gunboat Diplomacy and Freedom Cry. There was André Fabre's unbeaten three-year-old, Swain, and the filly, Carling − a true French *Cendrillon* − who had been bred by a farmer from a crippled dam, and risen from such beginnings to win the French Oaks.

Sixteen horses were to contest Europe's most glamorous and prestigious race, the Prix de l'Arc de Triomphe: the race towards which the season moves in awe. It was to be run on 1 October, a year and a day after the death of Alex Scott.

★

From childhood, I remember the Arc and its appearance on the television every year, after Sunday lunch, in the first weekend of October. From it, I first intuited the powerful remoteness of flat racing.

I remember, in particular, being at an adult party with my family at the age of about ten, and slipping away from its incomprehensible demands to the comfort of an empty bedroom and its portable television. There, on the screen, I found the Prix de l'Arc de Triomphe. Even more than the party I had just left, it seemed to be displaying itself to me from within a capsule of sophistication. The trees of the Bois de Boulogne were massed protectively around the horses, the crowd, the elegant white grandstand; beyond were the dusk and champagne colours of Paris.

A filly was favourite for the race that year. She too looked sophisticated: feminine, elegant, with a knowing slant to her eyes. Her name was Allez France. When she won the Arc, by a head, the Longchamp crowd greeted her like the conquering Napoleon; but still the tumultuous excitement remained within that mass of trees, that impenetrable sphere.

I knew the importance of the race from what Peter O'Sullevan was telling me, but I could have intuited that too, without hearing his words. It was there in the way the horses moved around the paddock, with that proud ability to inhabit space that the finest thoroughbreds have. It was there in the way that the crowd watched them, which, despite its Parisian self-possession, had an absorbed and respectful alertness. It was there in the attitude of the television programme itself, which conveyed, with that balance between ease and awe that the BBC keeps so well, the magnitude of the occasion. I could not help but know that this mattered.

The Arc, coming at the end of the season, had a different kind of grandeur from that of the Derby: more formal, more majestic. Its parading horses were not possibles, they were already certainties. They looked older, too. They carried with them their knowledge of the season and of seasons past: they had the set splendour of maturity, compared with the uncertain, tremulous beauty of youth. They did not enter the paddock shimmering with potential and future. They came to it with reputations, achievements, a real past. If the Derby was the race that could make a horse a king, then the Arc could turn a king into an emperor.

All the power of the season, generated by the Derby and the other great races, is collected within the Prix de l'Arc de Triomphe. On the first Sunday of October, that power masses itself within the trees of the Bois de Boulogne. Then it waits for one of the horses who, a few minutes earlier, paraded with its peers, to return to the paddock alone and in triumph.

The Arc was conceived in 1920 as the first truly international flat race: a horse from any country, and of any age, could compete in it. It was thought, at first, that it might only last for ten years. Its winning prize in 1920 was just twenty-five guineas. But within three years it had its first dual winner and first great champion – Ksar, who won the race in 1921 and 1922 – and so its status was confirmed almost immediately. In a stylish gesture of defiance, it was even run during the Nazi occupation, when the few horses in training were given ration cards.

Since its institution, the Arc has, in its turn, confirmed the status of most of the century's greatest horses. Ribot, the Italian champion, won it twice: in 1955, on his first race out of Italy, and in 1956, by what looks like further than the official six lengths. Sea Bird II won in 1965, the year of his ridiculous, cantering triumph over the Derby field. At Longchamp, he contested the Arc against four other Derby winners (the French, the Irish, the American and the Russian), the winner of the French Oaks and the subsequent winner of the Washington International. Sea Bird II's brief quickening in the final furlong won the race for him in a few seconds. After that he slowed again to a canter, finishing six lengths clear of perhaps the best field ever to contest the Prix de l'Arc de Triomphe.

His daughter, Allez France, won the race nine years later. Before that, of course, Nijinsky had lost by a head while, the following year, Mill Reef had won with considerable ease, setting a new course record. So too, in 1986, did Dancing Brave, the horse who won the Two Thousand Guineas, the King George VI and Queen Elizabeth Diamond Stakes, and the Coral-Eclipse Stakes, but had failed by half a length to catch Shahrastani in the Derby. Dancing Brave's Arc win is one of the most satisfying I have ever seen. Not because it vindicated his loss at Epsom — he was too good to need to do that — but because he ran, at Longchamp, the race that he *should* have run in the Derby. As before, he seemed in an almost impossible position when the field turned into the straight; as before, he began to move up on the outside, gaining ground all the time as he accelerated with glorious assurance. For a moment, within the final furlong, Dancing Brave gallops in a line with six fine horses, including Shahrastani and Bering, sire of Pennekamp. Then he simply continues past them: the decisive movement of greatness.

Since the institution of the Prix de l'Arc de Triomphe, other races have imitated its concept of the international race, vying with each other for ultimate value and prestige. The Arc became the world's richest race in 1949, but since then several have overtaken it. In 1995, its winning prize of £479,042 was slightly less than the Derby, and considerably less than several races outside Europe.

In 1996, the world's richest race was the newly inaugurated Dubai World Cup. Conceived and financed by the Al Maktoum family, it is run at the Nad Al Sheba course for total prize money of $4 million. It is not, however, an emulation of the Prix de l'Arc de Triomphe. It is run at the start rather than the end of the season; and serves a new and thrilling purpose, that of tempting all the best horses from the previous year to race against each other. It brings together kings and queens and emperors. It does not, as the Arc does, crown them.

Before the Dubai World Cup, the world's richest race was the Japan Cup, first run in 1981. In 1995, when it was run at the very end of the season, it carried a winning prize of £1.1 million, and was won by the German champion and Arc contender, Lando. Japan is keen to raise its status within the flat racing world, and many of Europe's finest horses – including Generous and Erhaab – have been sold for huge amounts to Japanese studs. However, the blood of these stallions has not yet permeated the racing itself. Although the Japan Cup carries considerable status, no decent European horse would regard winning it as a first priority.

The Breeders' Cup races, run in the USA, have more prestige, but they place European horses at such a disadvantage that racing, already a gamble, becomes in them at least doubly so. Some have triumphed over this: for example Alex Scott's Sheikh Albadou in 1991, Barathea in 1994 and, in 1995, the Irish filly, Ridgewood Pearl. She won a superb Breeders' Cup Mile, a race which is perhaps less problematical than some because it is, at least, run on grass.

No European horse, however, would have stood a chance against the five year old American, Cigar, who in 1995 won the £1 million Breeders' Cup Classic. He was a different order of horse altogether. Halling, who also ran in the race, was quenched by it: by the tough unsubtle riding, by the dirt track which caked his coat with grime, by the wet churning beneath his hooves. But Cigar loved it, all of it. Looking twice the size of every other horse in the race, kicking up dirt and showering it over himself with careless voluptuousness, he powered away from the field with an annihilating certainty that I have never seen in a European horse. He seemed to have an engine inside him, rather than heart and lungs. He was staggering: a man amongst boys.

It is impossible to know what would happen if he were to contest one of the European races, with their tactical running, their turf, their tricks and intricacies. It may be that he would annihilate the field again: certainly he looks capable of anything. His performance in the Breeders' Cup was the greatest that I saw in 1995. Yet it did not seem to belong to the world of flat racing that I understood. Indeed, it showed me precisely what I did understand by that world: how essential to me was its refinement.

American racing does not have this. It is all robustness, whereas racing is really a mixture of the two qualities. It sets the sport within a cruder context, which denies the aristocratic essence of the thoroughbred. It seems wrong, somehow, to see these horses pushed to the limit of their power – which, though vast, is also vulnerable – from the moment of leaving the stalls to the moment of passing the post. It seems wrong to see their polished bodies defiled with dirt. It seems wrong to judge them by American standards – those that demand victory, at all costs – without appreciation of their more secretive qualities, their mystery.

Cigar had mystery, most certainly he did; but not within that Belmont Park arena, which whooped in triumph at his power, his grit, his pioneer spirit, his disdain of frailty, his ability to win more races in a season than most European horses run in a lifetime. A great fire burned through Cigar. But the vital darkness within it, which flickers at the heart of flat racing, was overwhelmed by its all too naked flame.

A flat race is not a torch song, a display of lungs being drained empty. It is an aria: flowering and receding, casting little shadows as it grows, and waits, and crescendoes to its climax. It needs its refinements, and the thoroughbred that runs the race deserves them. As Sheikh Mohammed said: these horses are not machines, they are soul and flesh and blood. Treating them as such is the way to elicit their true nature – and, indeed, the true nature of their sport.

European race meetings may have their idiocies and affectations, but almost always they breathe the spirit of the thoroughbred. This, really, is the joy of attending them. You might see far more on the television, or in the betting shop; but wandering around those courses, on a brisk and sunlit afternoon, you can *feel* the horses. Their refinement and robustness is with you, in your body, head and heart. At the very best meetings, where everyone is breathing deeply and lovingly of this spirit, the communal, visceral understanding communicates itself outwards into the atmosphere. The air pushes and pulls and thickens. It acquires an astringent glamour, such as you might see in images of racing in Kenya during the 1940s, when the scented, earthy Happy Valley crowd drank deep from glasses of Krug into which, as they galloped by, the horses had drummed fragments of dirt.

This is the atmosphere of the Arc. It is a gorgeous thing to enter: it consumes, yet it also shrugs from you nonchalantly as you walk through it. Its smartness is instinctive and natural. The Longchamp course is pretty, not showy, and without the blatant segregations of the big English meetings. It has, too, the loveliest paddock I have ever seen – secretive, like the race itself, with the shadows of trees – and special because it is also the arena of triumph, to which the victorious horse will return.

Above all, there is the feeling of the city beyond. Despite the green leafiness of the Bois de Boulogne, you can almost smell the Gauloises in the air. The thin, evocative shape of the Eiffel Tower is printed beyond the trees, like a sketch upon the sky. The horses may run through what used to be a forest; but the Arc is an effusion of Parisian urbanity, as surely as Epsom and Ascot are displays of Englishness.

There have been racecourses in English cities, though these were hardly comparable with Longchamp. Alexandra Park, which closed in 1970, was a rough and ready London track at which the crowd could stand so close to the horses that the sense of their speed was almost overpowering; and, during the 1840s, there was a course across the hill on London's Ladbroke Grove. A road called Hippodrome Place indicates its position. It was closed because those attending meetings were continually mugged by gypsies, whose encampment was on nearby Pottery Lane.

But English flat racing has always, essentially, been in the possession of the countryside. The city goes to it, of course; but the sport's connection is always with those ancient and powerful images, in which horses run, nobly and eternally, across vast, untrammelled expanses of land. Paradoxically, this explains why the Arc exerts such a fascination over the English. It is not just the importance of the race; it is the unfamiliar thrill of horses running through a forest that is also *in a city*. It is irresistible, and all the more so because that city is Paris. For all the antagonism between the English and the French, there is also an unwilling mutual respect: and, to the English, the fact that this great race is run in a place that is both friend and enemy, both familiar and unfathomable, both romantic and remote, gives to the Arc a heady tang which is absolutely in the spirit of flat racing.

There is, indeed, a terrific competitiveness between the French and English horses in the race. The French have won it more times, as is to be expected; it is very, very hard for foreign horses to do so. Before 1995, no English horse had won the race since Carroll House in 1989. Longchamp is, in its way, almost as difficult to ride as Epsom, and it has its specialist jockeys in just the same way. There are some who think that Nijinsky may have lost the 1970 Arc because Lester Piggott, at that time inexperienced on the course, rode an inferior race to the winning French jockey, Yves Saint-Martin. Indeed it took Piggott several attempts to win his first Arc, on Rheingold in 1973.

The real problem with Longchamp is that it begins almost like a big handicap: the course is straight for the first furlong and a half, before curving round its first bend. Therefore, if a horse is drawn on the outside, it has either to be very much on the pace, or very much off it, in order to get to the rail and not be forced to run much further than it needs around the bend. Nijinsky, drawn fifteen and widest of the 1970 field, was taken to the rail at the back of the field as he ran along the straight. It was a position from which he was unable to extricate himself until perhaps too late: still tired from his victory in the St Leger, Nijinsky simply could not make up the ground on Saint-Martin's mount, Sassafras. He failed, though, by the barest inches. It is almost unbearable to see the closeness of his defeat. I have watched it many times on film, and I always think that he might just have made it.

Twenty-five years later, his son, Lammtarra, was drawn in the centre of the field and, in the English betting shops, he disputed favouritism for the Arc with Carnegie and Balanchine. There were concerns that, having won his Derby and King George on firm ground, he would dislike the softer turf at Longchamp. However, David Phipps says that 'the lads in the yard never worried about the ground in the Arc at all. We always thought he would handle it, because as a two-year-old he would always let himself down a bit better when there was a bit of give in the ground. Horses save themselves. You know, they're not as stupid as people might think. Lammtarra saved himself on the hard ground a bit. You know, he was cute.'

Frankie Dettori, though, had ridden Balanchine in her recent run at Longchamp, in which she was a narrow second to Carnegie, and had some doubts about whether he would prefer to ride her or Lammtarra in the Arc.

'Balanchine run very, very good in France. I thought: the old mare is back. And I'm sure that she loves the ground, and it left a little doubt in my mind. And I remember speaking to Sheikh Mohammed, and I said, I think the filly is coming strong. And he said to me: Frankie, stick with Lammtarra.

'And I do what the boss tells me to do, but I was kind of 50–50. It wasn't until Lammtarra's last piece of work – and, you know, usually he's very laid back at home, he does his own thing, plays around and just gets there and is happy to stay there. So his last piece of work, I *made* him work. I said, look, let's just concentrate a little bit. And he worked fan-tas-tic. And it was raining, the ground was a little bit soft, and I got off him and said: I'm *definitely* on the right one – !'

The ride on Balanchine then went to Walter Swinburn.

Dettori: 'So I don't know if I'll win the Arc, but I definitely know that he's better than Balanchine. I was very confident. But when I got up in the morning for the race, my hair was standing *five inch* from my skull. I remember walking down to reception, and there must have been a thousand English people there trying to get into the course. And they all had the *Racing Post*, and on the front is this picture of myself and Lammtarra – I thought, oh my God – ! And my hair went from five inch to *six inch* up.

'But once I got to the track I was relaxed. I spoke to my Dad that morning, and my Dad said, look, you're on the best horse. But the most important thing about the horse is make sure he jumps well. You can't afford to mess around, Longchamp's tricky, and he's only run three times. Make sure he jumps well, and ride him like . . . it's the Derby winner – !'

I had gone to the Prix de l'Arc de Triomphe in 1994, where I had seen my beloved Ezzoud run a fine fourth to Carnegie. The following year, I watched the race from my local betting shop. I had backed Strategic Choice as an each-way bet: I did not expect him to win, but I thought he might run second or third. I had no idea of whom I thought would win. It was as if my mind was paralysed on this point.

In the betting shop with me were a couple of old boys who looked like regulars, a rather grand old lady and a scattering of up-market young locals. They looked as though they knew little about the Arc, beyond the fact that it was a smart sporting occasion. This was proved when a girl in jeans and puffa jacket flounced up to the counter and said, in a clipped voice: 'I want to put money on

Carling. How do I do it?' The betting shop manager, showing her how to fill out a slip, said kindly: 'That's a topical name, isn't it?' (Will Carling's visits to Princess Diana at Kensington Palace had recently erupted into the news.) The girl in the puffa looked up from her writing, and stared at the betting shop manager in amazement. 'That's why I'm backing it,' she said, her little voice snapping like a Pekinese.

It was about half past three in the afternoon, a fine autumn Sunday. On the screens, Longchamp exuded the same proud, alert and nonchalant look that I remembered from twenty-one years earlier, when Allez France won the Arc. I was finding it hard to believe that the moment of judgement had arrived again. So weighted are these great races with expectation and memory, their reality is always a shock: squeezed almost to breathlessness by the significance that surrounds them.

I can remember little of how the horses looked in the paddock. I remember only the sensation of waiting, waiting, for something that would be truly magical, though I had no idea of what this thing was. I remember circular movements, and nodding, tugging heads, and taut rings of owners and trainers, and the pale, almost religious look of dedication upon the faces of the stable hands who led around their magnificent charges. I remember a slight feeling of sickness, which made no sense really, because I had no commitment to any of these horses: except, of course, Strategic Choice.

Certainly I do not remember that, as Frankie Dettori says, 'Lammtarra was being really tricky in the parade. He was very reluctant, he wanted to go the other way . . . so wherever he wanted to go, we went with him. I wasn't worried, because I knew he's done it before. But for outside people – they thought, maybe he's gone over the top.'

I did not think that: I thought nothing. The first thought that I remember having, a few furlongs into the race, was that Lammtarra was too near the front and could not possibly win. I had seen his

Derby, when he came from lengths off the pace in the final furlongs; and his King George, when again he went to the front in the
finishing straight. Here, I thought, he was certain to be overtaken.
He was second only to Luso, and seemed as though he would pass
him at any moment. I looked instead to Balanchine, well placed on
the rail, and to Carnegie, hanging on the outside; and to Strategic
Choice, who hovered behind Luso and Lammtarra.

I did not know that this was exactly the race that Dettori had intended to run.

'He jumped good – great. I chased him up for a furlong, I got
him running. I was in front, I was in front . . . then my pacemaker
Luso got to the front and I slotted in behind him. Our plan – !

'It was a strong pace, and we were going pretty fast. Really I was
the real pacemaker, because Luso was too far in front. I was the real
pacemaker. I was doing whatever I wanted to, you know. But
anyway, we came round the bend, and because we were going
quite strong pace, I automatically got him to slow down. Got him
to relax. Catch a little bit of energy back.'

Five furlongs out, as the race moved into the finishing straight,
Lammtarra took possession of the lead from Luso. At that moment,
and not one moment before, I believed that he would win the Prix
de l'Arc de Triomphe: and, from that moment, I wanted it more
than anything in the world.

'Luso came back to the field, and all the others bunched up
behind me. The others had to do what I wanted; but I did what I
wanted, for my horse. Was great. And we got into the straight, and
I got him balanced, and I said: right, let's go.'

With a bravery and decisiveness which now terrified me – as if it
was May again, and the Two Thousand Guineas, and Celtic Swing
moving into the lead to fulfil my dreams – Lammtarra hit the front
of the race like a bullet.

'France is one of those tracks where you can always get done by
horses with turn of foot. Because, somewhere along the line,

they're slowing up, and it doesn't become a true mile-and-a-half race. So that was the only fear I had in my mind: that I wasn't going fast enough, and that somebody would do me for turn of foot. Not because I wasn't good enough, but because they didn't even give him a chance to fight back.

'So I said: let's go and run. I got him going and – you just imagine. Lammtarra, right, he's come to Longchamp, he's in front, and the world's in front of him. All the crowd screaming left and right, all the speakers near the rail, no horses in front – so of course he was reluctant, you know – ! He didn't really want to go. It was different from what he'd experienced before. He had one ear pricked and one ear back, so I knew he wasn't giving me one hundred per cent.'

Yes – what it must have been like for him? To see the arch of triumph opening for him; to see the crowd on either side of it; but to feel that there was only him – and the clever little man on his back who understood him – in the world.

'So I gave him four backhanders, he's responded a little bit . . . and then I saw 'em coming.'

The two French horses, Swain and Freedom Cry, had moved up the field on to Lammtarra's outside. It all came up in me then: everything that I had felt, for almost a year now, since the Racing Post Trophy at Doncaster. I realised now that I had not backed Lammtarra for the Arc because I had wanted, simply, to let this moment happen. I crumpled up my betting slip. I did not want Strategic Choice to win this race; I did not care if he was second, third, or last; I wanted Lammtarra, Lammtarra, Lammtarra. And, with three full furlongs to go, the two French horses were by his side.

'I had to get a little bit serious with him. I give him ten backhanders. Then, when he saw the others coming, he thought: oh, shit. Let's run here.'

In the betting shop, I heard the voice of Peter O'Sullevan. 'It's Freedom Cry on the near side, who's taken it up from Lammtarra,' he said. The angle of the television camera made it impossible to tell whether he was right or wrong; from where I was sitting, or now standing, Lammtarra still looked to have the lead. But 'It's Freedom Cry,' said O'Sullevan, and again it was as if it were the Guineas, and another French horse moving past the one that I now so much, so much wanted to win.

'Freedom Cry never went by me. He never did. He got within a neck. But once Lammtarra saw horses coming, once he saw the competition – and with me being aggressive on him – then he started running. It was partly inexperience, that he let himself be caught, and partly . . . he enjoyed it. He enjoyed it.'

I was urging him on now, aware but unheeding of the appalled stares of the puffa jackets in the betting shop. 'Go on Frankie!' I kept muttering, pressing him forwards with my fist. 'Go on Frankie!' I did not know this horse; he was nothing to me, not even a name on a betting slip; but I felt now, with all my being, the rightness of this victory. And now Peter O'Sullevan was saying, 'Lammtarra's fighting back. It's Lammtarra taking it up again . . . Lammtarra's won it. Lammtarra's won it.'

And, as he passed the winning line, three-quarters of a length clear of Freedom Cry, then Swain, then Lando, with Balanchine and Carnegie and Strategic Choice lengths and lengths behind, I thought: Ah yes. So this is what was meant to happen. Lammtarra, after all, was the one.

This was where the pattern had led. The other names – Celtic Swing, Pennekamp, Tamure, Spectrum, Bahri, Pentire, Winged Love, Annus Mirabilis, Fahal, Riyadian, all the names that I could recite like a litany and that would forever remind me of the summer of 1995 – had been signposts on the road to greatness.

The accumulations of hope that had lain inside me since the spring had been forgotten at times, but I had remembered them again, with painful clarity, in the last half mile of the Prix de l'Arc de Triomphe. Now, at last, they dissolved as Lammtarra re-entered the paddock at Longchamp. Throughout the racing season, events had thwarted my desires and dreams; but, in the end, they had taken me back to them.

He knew what he had done. His dark eye was detached as ever, but within its self-possession glowed the sense of his own achievement. He was the most magnificent creature on earth at that moment, as Frankie Dettori leaped from his back and kissed him on the mouth. 'This horse is a lion,' said Dettori, who was streaming tears. 'He stays, he gallops, and he fights. He's the best we've seen in years.' He was a baby still, even now, with the schoolboy fringe falling loose across his forehead: a horse who had raced four times, for less than ten minutes, who had been learning how to race even in the last second of the Arc. But he was also the horse who had, after the months of frustration and uncertainty, fulfilled the racing season; and made its pattern clear at last.

And I, at last, had caught up with him. I had been unable to believe that a horse so different, in every possible way, from Celtic Swing could replace him on the road to greatness. Now I saw that Lammtarra could, and had. Now I gave to him all the feelings that had grown within me during the season's quest: every one of them converged now upon that impassive, sweating body.

Within the moment of winning the Prix de l'Arc de Triomphe, was contained the Derby, in which he had flown through the field, and the King George, in which he had borne down upon it, and the Arc itself, in which he had simply overmastered it. In that moment, as Lammtarra passed the winning post at Longchamp, I saw greatness: its chestnut coat gleaming, its green and white colours fluttering, its dark eye fixed upon it as it recognised it, at last, as its own possession. Then it was gone.

This was one end to the season. There was another, a couple of weeks later, that was a little different.

I was watching the last big race of the English season: the Dubai Champion Stakes. This is run over a mile and a quarter at Newmarket, and is sponsored by the Al Maktoum family. In 1970, it was Nijinsky's last race. He ran lifelessly, and finished a length and a half behind Lorenzaccio. Brigadier Gerard, superb as ever, won it in the two following years.

The 1995 field included Bahri, Spectrum, Tamure, Fahal, Riyadian and Environment Friend. As I watched them – the horses who had pointed the way to greatness – the season seemed to accumulate within their grouped and galloping bodies: not as it had when Lammtarra passed the line in the Arc, but with a softer, gentler movement.

The colours of their silks waved at me, like bright signifiers of the part that each horse had played in the season. I knew them so well by now, recognised them unthinkingly: Bahri's deep-blue and white striped cap, Tamure's maroon with white sleeves, Spectrum's pale, almost colourless blue with yellow cap, like the sky and sun of this October day. I knew what these horses had done. I had travelled through the season with them, and seen their triumphs, their near-triumphs, their failures.

I had seen Bahri lengths clear in the sensual heat of Royal Ascot, taken on his exhilarating journey beneath the trees in the Queen Elizabeth II Stakes, eclipsed by the pure sunlit dazzle of Halling at York. I had seen Tamure surge past Fahal for victory in the Derby; then seen both horses seem to stand still, even while they continued to gallop bravely, as Lammtarra flew past them. I had seen Spectrum hurt and defeated by that same race, unable to move from the back of the field: the place where those without hope in the Derby collect, but from which Lammtarra had glimpsed, then claimed, his impossible victory.

Through the glorious summer, these horses had revealed themselves to me. Yet, whatever I had learned about them during those months, I had learned something else more important: that their

171

mysteries can never be fully penetrated. Any one of them might, in this Champion Stakes, do something that he had never done before. Every fact that I held about them was infinitely plastic and manipulable. Did Bahri lose to Halling because Halling was a better horse, or because Bahri did not stay a mile and a quarter? Did Fahal have sufficient class to take advantage of his liking for the distance and the firm ground? Did Tamure or Spectrum have sufficient class to overcome their dislike of the ground? Did Tamure's recent defeat of Spectrum in France mean that Tamure was a better horse, or that Spectrum had then only been recovering his best form? There were no answers, before the race, to these questions. The horses held them to themselves.

But I remembered something that Spectrum's jockey, John Reid, had said about the horse – so many months ago now – which had led me to back him in the Derby. At the start of the season, he had said that, if there were no Celtic Swing, everyone would be talking about Spectrum. I knew that I would not be the only person who remembered this; nevertheless, *I* had done so. I had traced backwards through the pattern of my season and found this memory. It was *my* memory and through it I would, if Spectrum were to win the Champion Stakes, truly own my victory.

He did win the race. For me, it was a fitting second end to the season. I remember how strongly I felt this as, two furlongs out, a gap appeared in the wall of horses that barred Spectrum from the lead. For a second or two, his pale silks floated like a space amid the rich reds and blues; then he moved forwards. Yet it was not, as with Lammtarra, the moment of victory which gathered the season together. It was watching the procession of horses past the post: Spectrum – Riyadian – Fahal – Bahri – Tamure – Environment Friend: the horses who, after the Two Thousand Guineas snatched the season away from me, had rebuilt its framework and created its reality.

Even at the end of the Champion Stakes, when the particular

questions of that race had been answered, these horses still guarded the mystery of their kind. They were still remote, and refined, and unfathomable, and untouchable, but in my mind they had become my friends. They had, after all, taken me on the way to the greatest horse, and greatest mystery, of them all: Lammtarra.

IX

SIX WEEKS AFTER THE Prix de l'Arc de Triomphe, Ridgewood Pearl was voted 1995 Horse of the Year. It was a joke, really. She was a wonderful, wonderful filly: she had won the Irish One Thousand Guineas, the Coronation Stakes at Royal Ascot, the Prix du Moulin at Longchamp and, most impressively of all, the Breeders' Cup Mile in the USA. She was big and brave and beautiful. But there was only one Horse of the Year in 1995, and that was Lammtarra.

The fact that he did not receive the Cartier-sponsored award was particularly ridiculous, because the reasons behind it were so transparent. The Horse of the Year is judged on performances in Group races and by a panel of racing journalists; but it is also judged by votes from the racing public, and through these ran a thick stream of jealousy. Lammtarra did receive the three-year-old colt of the year award, but the racing public even voted Bahri ahead of him in the main category; though this was reasonable, considering that Bahri had beaten Ridgewood Pearl by six lengths at Ascot. Logically, in fact, Bahri could have been Horse of the Year, since he was the only horse to beat Ridgewood Pearl during 1995.

The jealousy that infected the desire to deny Lammtarra his due was, of course, directed towards the Al Maktoum family. Ridgewood Pearl, like Celtic Swing, was owned by 'ordinary' people:

Anne and Sean Coughlan, a likeable and accessible Irish couple, who brought water from Lourdes for their precious filly to drink. They were very different figures from the cabal of saturnine, impenetrable foreigners, who floated from success to success upon a sea of oil. It did not matter that this oil had helped to keep flat racing buoyant for the last fifteen years; that it also funded sponsorship and veterinary research, such as had saved the lives of Lammtarra and Balanchine. It did not matter that, for all their autocracy, the Al Maktoums could show great loyalty; as when Sheikh Hamdan gave horses and premises to Major Dick Hern after the trainer had been forced to leave his stables. It did not matter that, for every Lammtarra owned by the Al Maktoums, there were another forty or so horses that might not even win a Group race. All that mattered was that, in the opinion of some of the racing public, victory came to them too easily.

Of course, this feeling was compounded by the development of Godolphin Racing. In 1995, John Dunlop's first victory as champion trainer would always have been a popular one; but it was especially so in a year when, it seemed, Saeed bin Suroor was simply to be guided straight to the title by Sheikh Mohammed. In fact, Suroor lost it on the day that Bahri ran fifth in the Champion Stakes. The horse's £6,398 of prize money was enough to secure the championship for Dunlop. One of the first people to congratulate him was Suroor; so low had been his profile that Dunlop scarcely recognised him, but he was touched by the courteous gesture.

Resentment of Godolphin had simmered quietly for much of the season, as horses who had previously belonged to other trainers – Moonshell, Halling, Classic Cliché, Vettori and so on – floated with the Al Maktoums from classic win to Group win to classic win. However competitive these races may have been at the time of their running, it always seemed afterwards as though Godolphin victory had been inevitable.

Then, three days after the Arc, the quiet resentment boiled into fury when Sheikh Mohammed removed every one of his forty horses from the Warren Place yard of Henry Cecil. Shocking though this was, it had been presaged by a press conference, in which Sheikh Mohammed had criticised Cecil for allowing 'people who have no knowledge of horses to interfere with him'. This was interpreted as a reference to Cecil's second wife, Natalie, for whom he had left Julie, the daughter of trainer Sir Noel Murless and a much respected horsewoman in Newmarket. Sheikh Mohammed did not mention Natalie Cecil's name but he did not need to do so. 'Henry knows,' he said. 'Everyone knows. Newmarket knows.'

Natalie Cecil had protested against the removal to Godolphin of her husband's most promising two-year-old, Mark of Esteem. Considering that Cecil had, the previous season, lost three horses who subsequently won classics, any loyal wife might have found it hard to keep silent, but Sheikh Mohammed, who understands loyalty, did not understand that particular manifestation of it. No doubt this was not the first time that Natalie Cecil had said the wrong thing; no doubt Sheikh Mohammed is not a man who cares for outspokenness in women, especially those who have benefited from his wealth and patronage; but whatever finally caused him to come to his decision, the hard fact is that it was taken. On 4 October, it was announced that the partnership between the Sheikh and Henry Cecil had ended. It had produced some magical wins, notably from fillies: the exquisite grey, Indian Skimmer, who won the French Oaks and the Champion Stakes; and Oh So Sharp, one of the best horses of the last ten years, who won the One Thousand Guineas, the Oaks and the St Leger. But the Godolphin experiment, like Baron Frankenstein's, had assumed a life of its own. It had caused Sheikh Mohammed to turn remorselessly from this happy past, to a future in which he could pursue his personal quest for greatness.

His action caused a commotion in the press, as a rumpus amongst the privileged always will. Few people seemed to give much credit to Sheikh Mohammed's stated reason for removing his horses from Cecil. This was that Mark of Esteem had had a knee injury, of which the Sheikh had not been informed until the day that the horse was due to run; and which subsequently, in Dubai, was discovered to be far more serious than Cecil had ever implied. If this were the case – and there is no reason to think otherwise – then Sheikh Mohammed was more than entitled to his grievance. There was far greater interest, however, in the symbolism of what had happened than in the facts of it. On one side stood the trainer: charming, debonair, gentlemanly and English; the victim of a vast and spreading tyranny. Opposite him stood the owner: saturnine, hawkish, unyielding and alien; the man who had cast Walter Swinburn from Lammtarra's back; the man who, not content with ruling Dubai, now wanted to rule the racing world as well. Concentrated within their conflict was the whole, huge, insoluble problem of how to counter the supremacy and ambitions of Godolphin.

Eventually, of course, the *affaire Cecil* subsided, and it was realised that, as with the *affaire Swinburn*, Sheikh Mohammed would have had a proper, principled reason for doing what he did. No one does such things for the sake of it, especially a man who empathises so strongly with his horses. But Godolphin, and the symbolic power of what had happened, remained. So too did the memory of successes, the expectation of many more; and the illogical, yet understandable, resentment of it all.

How wrong, though, to let this jealousy affect judgement of racehorses: they, after all, have no control over who owns them. Yet in a strange way there was a jealousy of Lammtarra, as well as of his ownership. This was an obscure emotion, hard to define. It was there, though. There was no communal outflow of joy when the horse won the Arc and proved that 1995 had, after all, been a season which harboured greatness. There was, in fact, a certain relish of the fact that he did not receive the Horse of the Year award.

He should have run more, said his critics. He should have won his races by greater distances. He should have contested the Breeders' Cup, like Ridgewood Pearl did. He should have stayed in training as a four-year-old, instead of flouncing off to stud like a spoilt young gigolo. Don't blame us for voting against you, was the subtextual message to Lammtarra: it's your own fault.

When his record is compared with that of Ridgewood Pearl, it is, of course, superior. She won four, rather than three, Group One races, but Lammtarra's were unquestionably more prestigious: the three top middle distance races in Europe. That is unarguable. But Ridgewood Pearl won them differently. As she did so, she gave the public the sense that she was taking them with her. She had a charm, an openness, a way of displaying to the crowd the magnificence of what she was doing. She was an absolute Irish darling. She was, in fact, rather like Celtic Swing: the unexpected horse who becomes, through its talent and vitality, the expected one, the one in whom its public can do the thing that it so much longs to do: invest its emotions. And that, I believe, is why she won the Horse of the Year award. She, rather than Lammtarra, had become the popular replacement for Celtic Swing.

As *The Times* said: 'In nine out of ten instances, the most charismatic horse will be the best. Occasionally, however, that is not the case. The Cartier awards are all the better for acknowledging that fact.' In other words, Lammtarra was the best; but he was less charismatic than Ridgewood Pearl. He won the races, but he did not do so in the way that the racing public wanted him to. He was, in fact, too similar to the Al Maktoum family: too remote, too elusive, too protected. This is how the jealousy of his ownership came to be felt, implicitly, towards the horse as well; whilst, by a similar process, the liking for the Coughlans was transferred to Ridgewood Pearl.

Always, always, the attitude towards him was grudging. Not from a true racing journalist, like Geoff Lester, chief writer on the *Sporting Life*, who voted for Lammtarra as Horse of the Year; but, in general, he was not a horse who evoked a generous response. One article wrote of him 'preening at a Newmarket stud', which was a cruel and stupid thing to say. When the International Classifications were published, which judge the contenders within each season, he was rated the best European horse of 1995, though Cigar was overall champion. However, with a handicap figure of 130, Lammtarra was the ninth lowest top-rated horse of the last ten years. Derby winners Reference Point and Generous, who both failed to win the Arc, were classified above him, as were several horses who won none of the races in which Lammtarra had triumphed. Bahri, who had won only two Group One races and had been beaten easily by Celtic Swing, Pennekamp, Spectrum and Halling, was rated at 129, one point below Lammtarra.

This, too, was a joke. In its defence, the British Horseracing Board handicappers admitted that their system was extremely fallible; it had, after all, failed to rate Nashwan the top horse of 1989. But still the senior handicapper made a case – as, indeed, he had to – for the treatment of Lammtarra. He suggested that the opposition in the horse's three wins had not been top quality, and that the distances by which Lammtarra beat them did not, therefore, place him in the highest class.

This is an argument with which I can never deal. How on *earth* – I always want to say – can such a thing be gauged? How do you *know* that the horses beaten by Lammtarra are not top quality? The achievements of Pennekamp and Spectrum can be discounted, since they were unfit in the Derby; but Tamure and Presenting both won Group races. Pentire won the King Edward VII Stakes at Royal Ascot, the Great Voltigeur and the Irish Champion Stakes. Freedom Cry was a fine, brave second in the Breeders' Cup Turf. Winged Love won the Irish Derby, Strategic Choice the Irish St

Leger. Carling won the French Oaks, Pure Grain the Irish Oaks, Lando the Japan Cup. Carnegie won the 1994 Arc, Balanchine the 1994 Oaks and Irish Derby.

There are always arguments both for, and against, the quality of a horse. If every horse that ran second to Lammtarra had won a classic, it would still be possible to say that they, in their turn, had been beating mediocre opposition. It is very hard to find an absolute standard here. In the end, all that the horse can do is win. That is the criterion for judging Sea Bird II's Arc as the greatest twentieth-century victory: he was beating a field of winners. Lammtarra beat winners. Freedom Cry, who was second in the Arc and of whom it was said, by detractors, that he lacked the desire for victory, had in fact won twice during 1995. What more can these horses do?

Frankie Dettori: 'Everybody is really small-minded, and just looks at the distance between the first and second in the Arc. But if you look at the whole field, it's eighty lengths from the first to the last. They're spread out like . . . like flowers — ! Also Lando, Strategic Choice, Carnegie, Balanchine — they're mi-iles behind! That was a *great* performance from Lammtarra.'

David Phipps: 'It makes me mad when people say that Freedom Cry didn't want to win the Arc — he ran his guts out. I would never have expected Lammtarra to win his races by a large margin. I know people have knocked the horse — but how can you knock a horse that's run four times, and won four times, and three of the races are the biggest races in the world, that everybody that owns a racehorse would love to win?'

This, finally, is the point. One can quibble forever over niceties, over the fractions of a length which separate Lammtarra from Pentire and Freedom Cry. The irreducible truth is that the horse measured himself against the unforgiving judgement of the racing season: and its three greatest races pronounced him worthy of victory.

★

There was a sense, though, in which Lammtarra was regarded rather as if he were the young man in whose colours he ran, Saeed bin Maktoum Al Maktoum. They were the scions of privilege: the ones who had it all. They did not live within the world of struggle and disappointment and cold and anxiety. They moved from Epsom to Ascot to Longchamp without touching the grim banalities in between. For them, surely, nothing could ever be *that* difficult. As a Godolphin horse, under the supreme patronage of Sheikh Mohammed, Lammtarra had it easy; he could just emerge four times from his mink-lined stable, win the races, and then retire to a life of sex and luxury.

Of course, Lammtarra was protected within the world of the Al Maktoums. Their stables are, as David Phipps says, 'like five star hotels'; though Ridgewood Pearl would hardly have been living in a shack. It is also true that Lammtarra did not run in any race beyond the requirements of establishing his reputation. Commentators on the Horse of the Year award contrasted this with Ridgewood Pearl, who ran more often, and who contested the Breeders' Cup when she already had three Group One wins in Europe; though, in fact, the American race *was* the one that established her reputation. However, she did what Lammtarra did not do: she put on a show for her public. He did only what was absolutely necessary. He emerged four times, did what he had to do, then stopped.

But to imply that this in some way made what he did *easier* is beyond belief. It made it infinitely, unimaginably harder. Anyone knows that it is easier to hit a target four times from six or eight attempts at it, but Lammtarra had no near misses to perfect his aim. Four times out of four, he flew from the bow and landed on the bull's-eye.

Again, this staggering achievement has been attributed to some mysterious spell worked by Godolphin. Indeed, up to a point it should be: to bring any athlete to peak fitness at the right time is always a remarkable feat of training, and especially so when the peaks are so separate from each other. However, to suggest, as some

181

have done, that Godolphin horses are able to win any major race, without being prepared for it in smaller ones, is an absurd exaggeration. The winter in Dubai may advance a horse's preparation. It may make a full spring programme of races unnecessary. But, as I have said before, Godolphin are not magicians: they cannot put into a horse what is not there. A horse needs experience of European courses if it is to win on them, and the only way to get that is to run on them. The experience cannot be spirited into a horse with a waving wand.

Ah, but Lammtarra – ! who won the Derby ten months after a single, listed race over seven furlongs at Newbury, one of the easiest courses in the country. *He* did not need prep races. Godolphin, and the desert sun, must have prepared him instead.

They did: but they were preparing a great horse. As if another horse in a hundred thousand, maybe even in a million, could have done what Lammtarra did at Epsom! It could not, if that horse were owned by Allah himself. It was not a choice, or a decision, on the part of Godolphin to leave Lammtarra without experience when he ran the Derby. No choice was available. In the spring of 1995 the horse was dying. Preparatory races were not the issue; the issue was saving Lammtarra's life. It was hard necessity that left ten weeks, out of the ten months that elapsed between Newbury and Epsom, to prepare the horse for the hardest race in the world. The fact that Lammtarra triumphed over that necessity is, perhaps, the greatest achievement of all.

There were hints from Godolphin that Lammtarra might run in the Breeders' Cup, but these were never very convincing. On 11 October, it was announced that the horse would retire to Sheikh Mohammed's Dalham Hall Stud in Newmarket. Again, this was regarded as characteristic Al Maktoum behaviour. The racing public wanted to see Lammtarra run again: instead, he was to return, forever, to the protected sphere that he seemed so rarely to have left.

In fact, the removal to stud of fit young horses is far from being the preserve of the Al Maktoum family. In the 1930s, the then Aga Khan retired at the age of three his Triple Crown winner, Bahram, and Derby winner, Mahmoud; then, a few years later, sold both horses to the USA for huge sums of money, thus sending out of England some of this century's most influential blood (Mahmoud was the great-grandsire of the omnipotent stallion Northern Dancer, who stood at stud in Maryland). Forty years after this, the Robert Sangster syndicate inflated the value of stud fees to millions of pounds above that of prize money, thus making a retired horse a far more desirable property than a racing one. When a horse like Storm Bird could be sold for $28 million solely on the strength of his two-year-old form, where was the incentive to keep him in training? Indeed, during the years of Sangster domination, a horse's racing career became almost an irrelevance. Of course it had to win a couple of decent races, that went without saying; but once that was over and done with, the attention could go back to where it wanted to be: on the yearling sales and the stallion fees.

If, when a horse is running, its owner is seeing not a racing performance, but that of a potential stallion, then inevitably his attitude changes. He wants the horse to do as little as is necessary to establish its reputation. Above all, he does not want the horse to lose. An unbeaten record is worth millions at stud. In the early 1980s, a horse like Lammtarra might have been able to charge breeders $1 million a time to mate their mares to him.

Lammtarra's stud fee for 1996 matings is, in fact, £30,000. The days of Seattle Slew, an American horse whose fee *was* $1 million, are over; but the feeling persists that a horse should be protected from defeat in order to enhance its worth as a stallion, which is still far greater than anything it can earn in prize money. Many horses are still removed from the track the moment that they have done enough to merit a decent stud fee.

This trend, of protecting rather than testing ability, is not something peculiar to flat racing. Money has done it to other sports. Boxers are more adept at dodging each other out of the ring than inside it; athletes run against opposition that they feel sure of beating; greyhounds are prepared for only a few, carefully selected competitions each year. Quite simply, defeat is too expensive.

Yet, with Lammtarra, could this really matter? His owners were too rich, surely, to concern themselves with the financial risks of racing the horse as a four-year-old? Did he need to be protected in that way? If he lost a couple of races, and his stud fee went down to £20,000, the Al Maktoums were hardly going to be bankrupted. Why, then – asked the horse's critics – could Lammtarra not run again?

I should say that it was because there was something very valuable at risk in doing so. It was something far more precious than money, particularly for Sheikh Mohammed. Lammtarra represented something more than just an unbeaten record, and victories in the three most important middle distance races in Europe. He represented perfection.

That beautiful blood, running from the Darley Arabian through to Northern Dancer and Nijinsky. That self-contained magnificence of body. That silk and velvet chestnut coat. That dark and mysterious eye. That purity of breeding and conformation and demeanour; and, above all, of the four smooth, separate peaks of victory.

How could that be risked? How could Sheikh Mohammed, who had seen Derby victory in Lammtarra as the horse lay dying and struggling for breath, bear to touch that crystalline perfection? How could the temptation be resisted to remove it, with careful reverence, and place it within a setting where it could never be destroyed?

This perfection now shrouds Lammtarra like a cloth of gold. He is defined by it. When, in years to come, the racing season of 1995 is remembered, it will be for the horse who came and went like a spirit, leaving behind him those four pure peaks: like sunlit mountains in an empty landscape.

Yet this perfection was not just the possession of Lammtarra. It was the construct of human beings: the men who bred him, and nurtured him, and planned his career, and removed him from it, and ensured his unique place in racing history. It *was* perfection. But was it, also, greatness? What, in the end, does that word mean, when it is used to describe these horses?

I was never more certain of its meaning than when watching a recording of Sea Bird II. He is probably the closest that a horse has come, this century, to the earthly Pegasus. He did not win by the distances of old, yet you hear, quite clearly, the cry of 'Sea Bird first – the rest nowhere.'

He was not just a faster horse than the rest. He was too good for them. He was, perhaps, what we had wanted Celtic Swing to be. In our dreams, though, Celtic Swing would have done what Sea Bird did not bother to do. He would have run away from the others, pulling clear of them by lengths and lengths, and moved quite free and alone into his own, different world.

Like Eclipse and St Simon, Sea Bird was a freak horse. He was not notably handsome: a rich chestnut, with a streak down his face a little like Lammtarra's, and with two white stockings on his hind legs. He was bred and trained in France. His sire was unpredictable and inconsistent, and his dam never won a race. The grotesque truth is that she was £100-worth of butchers' meat before her great son had even raced: a second's glimpse of his ability would have saved her life. Nor was Sea Bird himself an especial success at stud. He threw Allez France and Gyr, second to Nijinsky in the Derby, but little else. He defied the rules of thoroughbreeding; though, of course, its first rule is that its rules can always be defied.

When I asked my father, who has seen many Derbies, which was the best winner that he ever saw, he spoke before he had even thought: 'Sea Bird.' I had not seen recordings of the horse then, was surprised by his answer and asked him why he had given it. 'Well, he didn't even have to try.' And that is what it looks like. A furlong out, he takes the lead with a sudden quickening that communicates itself, even through the television screen, like a breath of wind; then he slows to a canter, raises his head and pricks his ears, daring the rest even to try and catch him. He still wins by two lengths. It is impossible not to wonder what the distance might have been.

To run against him must have been miserably depressing. With any horse, however good, there is a possibility that it can be beaten; with Sea Bird this simply did not seem to exist. For what it's worth, his handicap rating of 145 is the highest ever given. In fact, he did lose once as a two-year-old, and my father even managed to back him at 9–2 for the Derby. In the last furlong of the race, he made bookmaking an irrelevance.

Yet his Arc was even more staggering; not just because he was beating such a fine field, but because of how he did it. It was so wayward, so disdainful of strategy or style. In the final furlong, he veered on a diagonal so sharp that he seemed almost to be running sideways. It took him right to the very centre of the course, and the amount of ground that he lost would have lost the race as well for another horse. Yet he was six lengths clear as he cantered towards the winning post. About a hundred yards from the line, his jockey knew that there was no need to try any longer; he took his hand from the rein, and reached down to stroke Sea Bird's neck.

About Sea Bird there could be no doubt, no doubt at all. He inhabited a different world. Nijinsky and Mill Reef did not do that; yet they, too, are regarded as great horses.

Partly this has to be because they ran so many races – many more than Sea Bird, who raced only eight times. Nijinsky did not just win the Triple Crown; he also won the Irish Derby, and contested the Arc and the Champion Stakes. Mill Reef won the Derby, the King George and the Arc; but he also won the Coral-Eclipse and, as a four-year-old, the Coronation Cup at Epsom. He would almost certainly have contested a second King George and Arc had not injury ended his career. Both horses were tested over a variety of distances – Mill Reef even won a high-class five furlong race as a two-year-old – and against a great many other horses. The only unanswered question is what would have happened had Nijinsky run as a four-year-old, and raced against Mill Reef.

For all that their names are coupled together, by the fact that they achieved similar feats in successive years, they were very different types of horses. Nijinsky – big, a deep bay, with an alert head on top of an unusually tall and beautiful neck – was a fiery, nervy animal. He had, as his trainer Vincent O'Brien said, 'a bit more zip than was good for his peace of mind'. His career was dramatic, superlative and exhausting. By his last two races it had left him ragged. Recordings show how he shies in distress from the wild attentions of the crowd, the strange cameras pushed into his face, the demands that, yet again, he prove to the racing world the greatness that he has already shown.

Mill Reef, in contrast, was a rather small, compact horse with an entirely equable nature. As my father says: 'I might be wrong, but I should say he's the only one of the really great horses that had no vice in him at all.' He gave everything to his races; not out of fear, or the desire to conquer, but out of a natural willingness to do the best of which he was capable. His victories are decisive – he won the Derby by two lengths, the King George by six, and the Arc by three – yet they never look showy. They have about them a look of benign, almost modest magnificence.

Mill Reef ended his career with victory, but soon afterwards he shattered his fetlock. There is some unbearably touching film of him struggling to walk – the great Mill Reef! – and more film of him accepting, with kindly patience, a clamour of childish hands upon his face. This is a scene impossible to imagine with Nijinsky at its centre.

But the records of the two horses, and the spectacular success that they both achieved at stud, bring them both to the same eventual place. They are not quite like Sea Bird, cantering derisively from the field. Nor are they perfect: Nijinsky had his two defeats, and Mill Reef, in an equally famous shock result, lost the Two Thousand Guineas to Brigadier Gerard. Yet they are great horses.

And since then? Dancing Brave? Nashwan? Shergar? Generous? Their achievements are comparable with those of Nijinsky and Mill Reef; yet no horses, since those two, seem to have gripped with quite such certainty the world of their sport. They had a consistency, a depth and range that travelled every inch, every moment of the racing season. They made it theirs, even in failure. So complete was their relationship with it, that not only are their names legendary within racing, but they are known by people who would recognise the name of no other flat racehorse.

Since then, greatness has become judged more subjectively. Most would say Dancing Brave; many would say Nashwan, Shergar and Generous. Some would say others. There comes a point when horses who have achieved similar feats cannot *all* be described as great. Then it becomes a matter not just of achievement, but of the relationship that a horse forms with the racing season, and with the public. Which brings me back not just to Nijinsky and Mill Reef, but to Celtic Swing, and to Lammtarra.

For both Nijinsky and Mill Reef, so strong was their relationship with the racing season, that an equally strong relationship developed between these two horses and the public. For Celtic Swing, the relationship with the public was stronger than that with the racing season. For Lammtarra, the opposite was true. Although he brought the 1995 season around to the place that it had tried to reach for so long, he could never be a replacement for Celtic Swing because he travelled through his journey alone. He had reached the destination before the public had even seen him move towards it. He did not take them with him; and, as the Horse of the Year vote shows, that is what many people want. That is what *I* wanted, from Celtic Swing. But what I learned, from him and from Lammtarra, is that the racing season is not like that. *It* takes its public on the journey. It took me to Lammtarra, when I was still trying to travel with Celtic Swing, and the fact that I discovered Lammtarra's true, full, magnificent worth, only at the moment of losing it, defines flat racing.

It is natural to seek allegiance; but it is natural to flat racing not to do so. Flat racing is not about allegiance. It is about the absolute ability of the supreme racing animal.

It may seem as though the popularity of Nijinsky and Mill Reef is proof of their greatness; yet, in fact, their popularity could not have had such range and depth, did it not proceed from the range and depth of their ability. It is wonderful to see the gentlemanly acknowledgement that Mill Reef gives to the loving applause of his audience. Without it, though, he would still have been Mill Reef. And it is horrible to hear the raucous screams of encouragement, which seem to fall upon the sweating Nijinsky like burning hail, as he dances uneasily to the stalls in the Champion Stakes. Here, as with Celtic Swing, was the overwhelming desire of the crowd to will events; and here, again, it caused the sport to assert itself with harsh, unbending stringency. Nijinsky, it implicitly said, as Lorenzaccio pulled away from him to cross the line a length and a half clear, might have done a damn sight better if he had been left to run alone, without the will of the crowd behind him.

Unlike Nijinsky and Mill Reef, Lammtarra did not travel every inch and moment of the racing season. He moved through it in the opposite way: the way that his name, 'invisible', implies. He travelled it almost in negative, revealing nothing, yet somehow ending the journey in triumph.

There is so much, still, that is not known about him. Every thoroughbred has its mystery: but his, unlike Nijinsky's and Mill Reef's, is a mystery within a mystery. What else was he capable of? What more was there within him? One of the strongest images that I retain of him is of those kicking, stamping hind legs after his first race at Newbury; their desperate desire to continue to feel the power that had run through them, like a spreading fire, for less than a minute. Now he would hold it within himself forever.

It was not until I talked to Lammtarra's two jockeys that I realised how extreme was the horse's inexperience, even in the moment of winning the Prix de l'Arc de Triomphe. I understood, then, that throughout every one of the five hundred or so seconds that comprised his career, he had been learning something new. I saw the size of the gap between his youth and his achievement. I admired him then, all the more; but I also wished, with a hopeless and wondering desire, that this gap might be closed a little more. Really I just wanted to see him again. I imagined a second King George, like Dahlia's; a second Arc, like Ribot's; the powerful conversion of the will of the crowd.

When Lammtarra was retired to stud, the official Godolphin statement was that the horse had 'nothing left to prove'. In one sense, of course, it was true. How could a horse need to do more than win Europe's three most important races? Yet there was also the other sense: of all that was left within Lammtarra, all that power which would never, now, be seen or known. That, still, was left to prove.

Frankie Dettori, who rode Balanchine, Barathea and Lochsong, says that Lammtarra was 'the best horse I've ever ridden'. Then he says: 'And I don't think we've seen the best of him. I think we've only seen eighty-five per cent. And that's a shame. But he's won everything, and it would have been a bigger shame if he would have broke down in the track. So I'm pretty happy that he's gone to stud.'

David Phipps: 'I'm sure as a four-year-old he would have developed better. But whether he'd have *been* better – we'll never know.'

Julia Scott: 'It's nice to have that unbeaten record, but when he's only run four times I think it's a bit of a shame. And also, the press don't talk about him as one of the greats, whereas if he'd gone on the next year he might have been one of the greats of all time. I mean, you never know, do you?'

There were rumours that Lammtarra's early retirement may have been forced by his temperament. Though perhaps less quick and nervy than his father, he was, like him, a clever horse, alert and easily bored. He had his own thoughts and, unlike Mill Reef's, they were not always beautiful ones. As Julia Scott says, he had been 'a bit of a monkey on the gallops' from the first; his stubbornness is something to which everyone testifies. But while he was learning, and his intelligence was being satisfied, he was willing to do what was required. Frankie Dettori describes this:

'The horse just needed you to tell him what to do. And he was very co-operative with that, you know. Some horses are very reluctant, and some are very dopey, they take a long time to learn. But him' – he clicks his fingers – 'he learned straightaway. That was what was so remarkable about him. He had the ability, and he had the ability to learn.'

Within the rumours about Lammtarra, though, was a hint that, once he felt there was nothing more for him to learn, he would stop trying to do so. They are only rumours; but they make a certain sense. Throughout his career, Lammtarra was fascinated by what he was doing. Everything was new: the Newbury race, in which he could barely run in a straight line; the Derby, in which he had to extricate himself from a knot of horses; the King George, in which he had to beat off the threat on his shoulder; the Arc, in which he had to run alone through the wide arch of triumph. It was all a challenge, all a fight; and, as Dettori says, he enjoyed it.

When it no longer held that newness, that sense of windows opening on to absolute freshness, would he still have enjoyed it? After all, he had already done what he had done.

Comparisons with Nijinsky and Mill Reef are, therefore, impossible. Everything is as different as it could be. In the end, there are only the records; and these, of course, *are* comparable. Only Lammtarra and Mill Reef have won the three great races of Europe. Only Nijinsky came so close to doing so. Beyond that, who knows what would have happened had Lammtarra run against them?

David Phipps: 'It's very hard to compare. You know, the other two did a lot more racing. They were bloody good horses. And Lammtarra was a bloody good horse. If they were both here now, you wouldn't be scared for him to take them on, would you?'

I liked that: that acceptance of the fact that a horse can come upon greatness by stealth, as well as by show. Of course it is impossible to feel about Lammtarra the way one feels about Nijinsky and Mill Reef, who gave themselves again and again, measuring themselves against the racing season until, in the end, and in their different ways, they were defeated by it. This never happened to Lammtarra. He ended as he had begun: wrapped in the golden cloth of perfection. Until he lost a race, no one could begin to fathom the depths of his ability and will. And this was something that, for all my desire to see him run again, I did not want to happen; not within a world that was waiting for it, waiting to know that he was not, after all, another Nijinsky or Mill Reef. Let the perfection gleam in its setting forever.

Somehow, though, I could never have imagined him in defeat. Not because it has never happened; but because I cannot help but feel that he would, somehow, have flown, or pushed, or held his way to the line. For he was a brave horse. That, as much as perfection, defined him. His will, like his power, was unfathomable. His four victories form their smooth, sunlit peaks; but their faces were rocky and treacherous to climb. Lammtarra fought for life. He fought to run in the Derby, and he fought in it for victory. He fought, too, for the King George and the Arc. When Pentire and Freedom Cry hung upon his shoulder, casting shadows upon the gleam of triumph, he fought them away from him. His head did not strain forwards in agony, like those of Bustino and Grundy when they battled to the line in their 1975 King George. He did not show courage being pulled from him, inch by painful inch. It was buried too deeply within him for display; it invited neither sympathy nor pity.

Quite simply, he gave however much courage it took, in order to do what he had to do. He did, as always, whatever was necessary; then kept the rest to himself.

Although comparisons with Nijinsky and Mill Reef falter, there is something about Sea Bird that reminds me of Lammtarra. Both have an absolute opacity. Both conceal a power whose depth can only be guessed at. Both are like the spirit of a horse, rather than a horse itself: for all their magnificence, they convey only a blank impersonality as they run, impossibly at odds with what they are doing. However great the emotions that they arouse, except for the most fleeting of moments these are refused their full expression.

With those two horses, whose remoteness is so absolute, I feel an extreme bafflement. Ultimately, though, it is a feeling that I have with all the great horses: even Mill Reef, with his kindly nods, and Nijinsky, with his admissions of defeat. This is how, in the end, I know in myself that these *are* great horses: because I know the feeling that they arouse in me.

Even in memory, and within the safety of the past, they still do so. Watching a race that has already happened is, of course, very different from watching it in the present. The emotions that the race evokes are sweeter and deeper, as, over and over again, that unconscious flame possesses the horse – 'Lammtarra's coming from another county' – and it moves towards my knowledge of what will happen. Then I have, in a way, the advantage of the horse.

I am no longer at the mercy of its unpredictability. I have the space, and the control, to express the weight of emotion that these fragile races conjure, but cannot support.

Yet even the accumulations of time cannot gather, within a deadening softness, the moments in which greatness shows itself. I wish in a way that they could. These are not happy moments: I put off watching a video of Nijinsky for a month after buying it, because I could not bear to confront the glory of the horse. But they are moments that we all need, without which life is a dreary thing. They are not to be shared or even, particularly, enjoyed. They are about standing, alone, before something created by the world when it was stretched to its utmost: as it was when it made a thoroughbred racehorse so great that it could triumph over its own, aristocratic kind.

These are the moments that illumine the rest of life. So absolute, though, is their brightness, that they also make life's shadows clearer: too clear. This is why they are not happy moments. They demand and reveal too much. They demand a movement towards them, and reveal how nearly impossible this is. They are magnificent; but they are also painful, and baffling, and as hard to leave as they are to confront. They are like staring up into the faces of statues from the ancient world. Within that marble smoothness is nothing familiar or intimate, nothing that allows an easy human recognition. There is, instead, something larger and simpler: an impassive understanding of life's mysterious grandeur.

Greatness is not thought of as a moment. We speak of a great novel; a great symphony; even a great horse race. Always, though, these converge upon moments: the ones in which we recognise their greatness within us. The moment in which Macbeth stares at his blood-stained hands; in which Nijinsky the dancer leaps airily across the stage in *La Spectre de la Rose*; or whatever it may be: moments which live in an eternal and perfect present.

For Nijinsky the racehorse is not dead, when he lifts his neck in that high flourish after winning the 1970 King George. Nor is Mill Reef, when he passes the line in the 1971 Arc, and acknowledges the crowd with such benign magnificence. And as for Sea Bird, pricking his ears as he canters up for his 1965 Derby . . . Even Shergar is not dead, galloping ten lengths clear of the field at Epsom, on a joyful young summer day in 1981.

And then there is the moment in 1995 when Lammtarra won the Arc, and I thought to myself: Ah yes. This is what was meant to happen. A moment of greatness, a shining peak, converging above the unfathomable depths.

Time does not change this, but it does change something about greatness. It establishes it in the world of legend. Certainly time did this to Nijinsky. In 1970, when he retired to stud, there were those who did not accord him greatness. Phil Bull, who conceived the *Timeform* racing guide, said that, whereas Sea Bird was a great horse, Nijinsky's two defeats meant that he could only be considered a 'very, very good' horse. It shocked me to read this, since I cannot remember a world in which the legend of Nijinsky's greatness did not exist. But, over time, the private communion that thousands of people had formed with the horse opened itself out; gradually, it merged into something public; finally, it became an article of faith. There may be those who do not think of Nijinsky as a great horse, but they keep their opinions very, very quiet.

It may be, too, that time will confer a common belief in the greatness of Nijinsky's finest son. 'Everyone knows that he is the greatest horse of a generation,' says Frankie Dettori, 'and eventually everyone will *say* that he is.'

Lammtarra is defined by perfection, and he is defined by bravery, but he is also defined by the nature of flat racing; and this, as I have learned, is not always easy to accept. In Lammtarra, I felt the essence of his sport: the pull between the refined and the robust, between the ephemeral and the enduring, between the arousal and denial of human emotion. And I felt, too, that magnificent and painful pull upon my heart, as I watched him run towards a winning post, with his dark eye fixed upon the mystery of greatness.

X

I WAS STANDING AGAIN before Marcus Aurelius's horse, except that this time he breathed, and blinked, and smelled faintly of dung and straw. Again, I felt that if I wanted to fathom this sight, I would have to stand there for the rest of my life.

I had been oddly calm as I drove to see Lammtarra at Dalham Hall Stud. This was because I knew that there could be no disappointment. I knew how it would feel to stand before greatness; Lammtarra, at last, would be just as I expected.

I wandered round Newmarket before seeing the horse, and felt how naturally the sport of racing forms a part of England. It is everywhere in this town: in the great Heath, on which the horses gallop, which seems both to spread away from you and engulf you; in the broad, rough sweep of the Rowley Mile racecourse; in the elegant headquarters of the Jockey Club, which dominate the High Street; in the signs for saddlers and horse feeds, which punctuate every road in the town.

There is, in Newmarket, a sense of unquestioning, unspoken purpose. So deeply does this permeate that it does not need to be exhibited: most towns to which fame is attached are, like Stratford, choked by the demands of tradition and presentation, but Newmarket is far too busy getting on with the job. Its memories require no conscious display. They are alive, all around it, in the shape of the animals which gallop across the Heath twice every day. In its complete communion with the horse and its sport, and its consequent simple self-assurance, it is unlike any other town. It is as different as can be imagined from the aimless constructs of the late twentieth century, whose shopping centres and paved, flowery walkways are intent, it seems, only upon recreating a house and a garden for people who are bored by their own.

The road that led to the stud itself was lined with stables. Beyond, I saw the occasional group of grazing mares. This was out of the flat racing season, so the power that lies within Newmarket was revving very quietly. But the merest glimpse of horses could remind me of how close I had come to their reality, their world, rather than the presentation of it that I saw at race meetings. Here were no bright silks, fluttering in the sun; no hollering crowds; no Great Exhibitions of the English Character. Here were people who understood, as nearly as was possible, the mysteries of the thoroughbred horse. They had the instincts of Alexander the Great who, when told that he would never tame the untractable Bucephalus, intuited that the horse was frightened of his own huge shadow, turned his head towards the sun and rode him from that moment on.

As I approached Dalham Hall, passing fields and trees and the mares beyond, I conjured images of horses who were free to graze and run and group. I thought of fine racing fillies who, when they gave birth, acquired a look of calm, watchful fulfilment. I thought of the foals themselves, their legs almost as long as those of colts, daring to break away from their dams into short, stilted, joyful runs. I thought of yearlings, standing together in line with their long, slim heads staring out from over a fence. I thought, too, of a few moments of film that I had seen of Nijinsky, in which he ran alone around a paddock. Sometimes trotting, sometimes plunging into a sudden curving gallop, he took possession of his surroundings, fully, and in whatever way he pleased. As he did so, with the high folds of his ears turning little circles, his body seemed to make the shapes of his Arabian ancestors. His tall neck curved in delight, his black mane flourished, and the tense imminence of the racing horse fell away from him.

The drive up to Dalham Hall is a long and imposing one. Marked as it is by signposts to other studs owned by Sheikh Mohammed – Church Hall Farm, Derisley, Hadrian – and to the various offices and units within Dalham Hall itself, it is part of a world of its own. It feels as spacious as an empty town, yet massed within it is the sense of wealth and privilege.

The air of purpose that Newmarket holds with such ease is re-flected here, then strengthened to an absolute intensity. Everything is directed towards a single aim: that of producing a great racehorse. Everything is functional, labelled, supremely and satisfyingly organ-ised. There is a foaling unit, which the stud workers can watch on closed circuit television, and from which – even though it was empty when I visited – emanates a quiet protectiveness. There is, too, a covering barn where, between the months of February and July, the stallions are taken to mount the mares. The most successful of them might cover three in a day, and as many as sixty-six in a season. The barn in which they do so is vast and circular, like an arena. It is dimly lit and thickly padded, so that no agitated horse can fly against the walls and injure itself. In its centre, like a small stage, is a mound: upon it stand the shorter horses, and the mares who are covered by unusually tall horses.

The stallions standing at Dalham Hall are stabled, in a courtyard, around the corner from the covering barn. There were eleven of them at the time of my visit. They included Machiavellian, the lead-ing European first season sire in 1994, and father of Vettori; Shareef Dancer, then fifteen years of age, the Irish Derby winner for whom Sheikh Mohammed and Robert Sangster had bid with such de-termination; and Arazi, the dazzling champion two-year-old of

1991. As I moved beneath the arch that led to them, the close sense of wealth and privilege, which the covering barn — so dark, yet so businesslike — had sharpened with a strange eroticism, became possessed by something greater: a sense of awe.

There was such a stillness about this courtyard, with its handsome boxes, on whose walls are hung shining plaques, detailing each stallion's bloodline. The stillness was created by the stallions. It was threatened each time one of them made a faint, restive shift upon their hooves. I knew that within these boxes stood millions of pounds worth of bloodstock. That knowledge partly created the sense of awe, but it was something far more than that: it was a knowledge of the force that lay, quiescent, within these quietly rustling horses. The first glimpse I had of one of them was when I passed the box of Arazi. He was nothing more to me than a chestnut back, slung across with a rich, red rug. He stood in his box like a statue. But his unnatural stillness, which held the knowledge of being watched, held too a pure concentration of power.

Arazi was six at that time. I had been unprepared for the physical difference between a horse of that age, and a colt of three or four. When the stable door was opened for me to enter the box of Lion Cavern, a six-year-old stallion, whose dark chestnut coat was roughening for the winter, I was shocked by his size and splendour. He would have been scarcely taller than a colt, but everything about him was richer, deeper, thicker; higher in its arches, fuller in its curves. His body seemed, indeed, to have acquired another dimension. The crest of his neck rose like a great, ragged wave. The swell of his ribs and quarters pushed outwards, tight as vast drums. Every sudden shake of his head, or tentative raising of a hoof, or flick of an ear, was a small explosion of danger. His eye, rolling above mine, showed white with roguish threat: he was becoming restless. The covering season would begin again soon, and he sensed its approach. By June of next year he would be bored by it; now, though, he was bored with waiting for it, with the calm routine of leisurely exercise. He was a real man of a horse, and an entirely different creature from the slender, callow athletes that run through the racing season.

It was hard to imagine that Lammtarra would ever look like that. In my mind, he was a wraith-like animal, with his bruised eye, his light coat and his long, lean, outstretched body. This was how I thought of him, as the spirit of a great horse, at the end of his invisible journey towards greatness.

But his coat was glowing with fires: it was warm to see, and warm to touch. It was silky, too, as a child's skin, particularly in the slender, secret hollow beneath his neck.

There, before me, was the straight schoolboy fringe which I knew so well. There was the thin, trickling tear between the eyes, which I could trace now with a finger. There was his name, engraved on the bridle that he wore. This was him, Lammtarra; not a spirit, but a real, warm, silky horse, who smelled faintly of dung and straw: the horse that I had watched become speed incarnate in the Derby, that had fulfilled my childish, hopeful dreams in the Prix de l'Arc de Triomphe. This was the horse whose greatness I had discovered, not through legend and hearsay, but for myself: the first great horse that, in my own mysterious heart, belonged to me.

He was easing himself, gently, on a bandaged hoof. That, and a tiny nick in the skin of his back, were like the betrayals of his perfection.

After Lion Cavern, the youth of Lammtarra seemed to glow through his warm silky coat, and the rounded diamonds of his eyes. 'He's a baby,' said the man who showed him to me, smiling patiently at my wondering eyes and hands. 'But he's easing down, settling in well . . . he'll make a really nice horse.' He was already losing the look of a racer; the slow rhythms of his retirement causing him to thicken a little beneath the ribs. I thought then of the brief perfection of his career, and the power of those stamping, kicking hind legs. There they were now, in front of me. Were they yearning to unleash themselves again?

Did Lammtarra regret that he would never again be forced to test himself, against the magnificent, unyielding rigour of the racing season? Or would he be glad to run free, like Nijinsky in my moments of film, plunging and curving in the shapes of his Arabian ancestors? We were directing him now to a new purpose: that of propagating greatness like his own. Would this life replace, for him, the memories of urgency and clamour, of the fiery little men upon his back, of the great horse bodies jostling and sweating around him? What would he do with the memory of how he had looked into the depths of his own courage and will, and heard the sound of his own hooves as they ran towards greatness?

He eased himself, again, on one of those hooves. He had not looked at me. He was looking in my direction, but his eyes were glancing across mine; like those of Marcus Aurelius's horse, and those of every thoroughbred aristocrat that I had ever stared at, in awe and amazement, in a racecourse paddock.

Now I was starting to feel the pain that came with the magnificence of greatness. I had touched Lammtarra, who, for a few moments, had become just a real, young, beautiful animal; now I was putting my face on to his, feeling the smooth coat that still believed it was in the warmth of the desert; but I could not penetrate his mystery. The long, slender, tapering lines of his head were bearing down upon mine like those in the skeleton of Eclipse, which I had seen earlier in the National Horseracing Museum in Newmarket. They were the same blood; the same kind; and even when they turned to bones they held their secrets.

It seemed strange, somehow, that this was where the quest for greatness ended: in a place of such stillness and quiet. I found it hard to leave, and hard to realise that what I had found in Lammtarra, in the last moments of the Prix de l'Arc de Triomphe, was now locked forever behind the door of a stallion box. How could I move on to the new quest, when the paddock at Longchamp was still imprinted with the pattern of Lammtarra's hooves?

To think of what was to come, though, made me long to immerse myself again in the rhythms and mysteries of the new season. All the meetings that were now just lists in the racing calendar would bloom with life, unfolding and flourishing like the summer that they had almost come to define. These names helped to trace the pattern of the year, running as they did through its heart: Doncaster – Newbury – Newmarket – Chantilly – Epsom – Royal Ascot – Newmarket – Ascot – Goodwood – York – Doncaster – Longchamp – Newmarket: with them came the changing colours of the sky, the glamorous reign of the sun.

With them, too, would come the return of familiar horses, and the emergence of others who would push up through the season like new springs in the fountain. Each would bring their own particular joy: the moments of magic that could be anticipated, and those that would come unexpectedly. I knew, at that time, that I could look forward to the emergence of Alhaarth, Blue Duster and Bosra Sham, and perhaps to the return of Pentire, Pennekamp and Spectrum – even of Celtic Swing. I also knew that there would be others whose capacity to surprise would be almost infinite. That was what I had learned from the 1995 season, and from Lammtarra. They had revealed with extreme, perhaps unprecedented, clarity an essential truth about flat racing: that only the races themselves can begin and end the quest for greatness.

I did not expect to find another Lammtarra in the following season. I did not expect, in fact, ever to find another Lammtarra. How could the pure, formal simplicity of that story ever be told again: the story of the chestnut changeling, of the season which had looked with such assurance to one horse, only to find, as the curtain fell, that his role had been assumed by another? How could there be another horse like Lammtarra, sketching his four swift peaks of greatness, then dropping the pencil as he flew from the arena? Would a horse ever, again, erupt into the season in quite the same way? Would a horse ever, again, be quite so cool, quite so opaque, quite so mysterious?

The next one would do it in his or her own way. It might be a way that other people would prefer but which, inside me, would create a less intense quickening spark. That did not matter. What mattered was that it would, beyond doubt, happen again: that from inside the stallion box, the setting which protected and displayed Lammtarra's perfection, and proclaimed on the wall the pure lines of his ancestry, the quest for greatness continued.

As I walked away from him, my hands still held the silky warmth of the hollow beneath his neck, and the horse smell of him was still in my nose.

Then I went back. I wanted to look just once more. He was turned resolutely away, munching deliberately from his stall; he seemed, as Arazi had done, to be aware of a presence. I longed for him to look around. But this was Lammtarra who had turned away, Lammtarra who was doing what he wanted to do. I would have expected nothing else; nor would I have wanted it.

As I myself turned away, however, and moved almost beyond where he and I could see each other, he did look around. I saw a taut, upright ear, and a smooth, young, diamond eye, gleaming almost blue in the shadows and seeking out mine. The look in it was extraordinary. 'I know what you think of me,' that look said. 'But you don't know the half of it.'

Appendix and Index

LAMMTARRA'S FOUR VICTORIES

The Aristo Washington Singer Stakes (Listed)
Run at Newbury on 12 August 1994
£8,773
Seven furlongs, for two-year-olds

1. LAMMTARRA (USA) (Saeed bin Maktoum Al Maktoum)
   Ch c Nijinsky–   *Saeed bin Suroor*   8 8
      Snow Bride   Emerald green, white   W. R. Swinburn
                      chevron, striped
                      sleeves

2. MYSELF   *P. Chapple-Hyam*   8 9
                                              J. Reid

3. PETOSKIN   *R. Hannon*   9 0
                                              B. Raymond

Distances: ¾ length; ¾ length; 6 lengths
S.P.: 3–1; evens; 16–1. Favourite: Myself
Race time: 1 minute 28.26
4th Daffaq; 5th Wigberto; 6th Sarasota Storm

The Vodafone Derby Stakes (Group One)
Run at Epsom on 10 June 1995
£504,500
One mile about four furlongs, for three-year-olds

1. LAMMTARRA		9 0	
		W. R. Swinburn	
2. TAMURE	J. Gosden	9 0	
		L. Dettori	
3. PRESENTING	J. Gosden	9 0	
		C. Asmussen	

Distances: 1 length; ¾ length; 1¼ lengths
S. P.: 14–1; 9–1; 12–1. Favourite: Pennekamp 11–8
Race time: 2 minutes 32.31 (course record)
4th Fahal; 5th Court of Honour; 6th Vettori; 7th Riyadian; 8th
Humbel; 9th Munwar; 10th Salmon Ladder; 11th Pennekamp; 12th
Korambi; 13th Spectrum; 14th Daffaq; 15th Maralinga

The De Beers King George VI and Queen Elizabeth Diamond
Stakes (Group One)
Run at Ascot on 22 July 1995
£278,760
One mile four furlongs, for all-aged horses

1. LAMMTARRA

3 8 9
L. Dettori

2. PENTIRE   G. Wragg   3 8 9
M. Hills

3. STRATEGIC CHOICE   P. Cole   4 9 7
T. Quinn

Distances: Neck; 1½ lengths; head
S. P.: 9–4; 3–1; 25–1. Favourite: Lammtarra
Race time: 2 minutes 31.01
4th Winged Love; 5th Broadway Flyer; 6th Carnegie; 7th
Environment Friend

The Forte Prix de l'Arc de Triomphe (Group One)
Run at Longchamp on 1 October 1995
£479,042
One mile four furlongs, for all-aged horses

1. LAMMTARRA		3	8	11
		L. Dettori		
2. FREEDOM CRY	A. Fabre	4	9	5
		O. Peslier		
3. SWAIN	A. Fabre	3	8	11
		M. Kinane		

Distances: ¾ length; 2 lengths; 1½ lengths
S. P.: Pari-mutuel 3.10; 2.20; 3.90. Favourite: Lammtarra
Race time: 2 minutes 31.80
4th Lando; 5th Pure Grain; 6th Carnegie; 7th Partipral; 8th
Gunboat Diplomacy; 9th Carling; 10th Balanchine; 11th El Tenor;
12th Tot ou Tard; 13th Luso; 14th Strategic Choice; 15th El
Sembrador; 16th Sunrise Song

INDEX

General Index

Starkey, Greville 46
Stoute, Michael 40, 41
Suroor, Saeed bin 54–55, 79, 175
Swinburn, Walter (senior) 139
Swinburn, Walter 24–7, 46–51, 63, 68, 79,
    105–7, 109–10, 128, 135, 136, 138–9,
    144, 148, 165, 177

Tesio, Federico 92
Thompson, Derek 92
Timeform 9, 71, 195
The Times 72–3, 141, 178
2000 Guineas 1, 4, 14, 16, 28, 29, 30, 32, 46, 71–6,
    77, 78, 79, 80, 81, 85, 112, 117–18, 131,
    147, 153, 154, 159, 167, 169, 172, 188

Washington International 142, 158
Washington Singer Stakes (*see also*
    Lammtarra) 28–29, 30, 37, 46–51, 68,
    120, 148, 182, 190
Wilson, Julian 133
Wokingham Stakes Handicap 114
Wolverhampton 8

York 11, 86, 151–2
Yorkshire Oaks 35, 156

Horses

Alhaarth 153, 155, 203
Aliysa 15
Allez France 157, 159, 166, 185
Annus Mirabilis 31, 118, 124, 152, 169
Arazi 199–200, 204
Awaasif 35

Bahram 2, 183
Bahri 71, 72, 74, 76, 118, 121, 133, 152,
    154–5, 169, 171–2, 174, 175, 179
Balanchine 52–5, 68, 119–20, 136, 156,
    164–5, 167, 169, 175, 180, 190
Ballydoyle 39
Barathea 136, 160, 190
Bering 80, 159
Blue Duster 121, 153, 203
Blue Wind 139
Blushing Groom 35, 46
Bosra Sham 153, 203
Brigadier Gerard 27, 73, 140, 143, 171,
    188
Broadway Flyer 140, 145–8
Brown Jack 65, 130
Bustino 143–144, 193
Byerley Turk 11–13

Cadeaux Genereux 42, 46
Carling 156, 166, 180

Carnegie 29, 76, 140, 145–7, 156, 164–5,
    167, 169, 180
Carroll House 163
Celtic Ring 33
Celtic Swing 19, 28, 29, 31–4, 35, 37, 64–7,
    69–84, 85, 91, 92, 93, 96, 109, 112,
    117–18, 121, 122, 123–6, 130, 141,
    145, 147, 152, 153, 155, 167, 169–70,
    172, 174, 178, 179, 185, 188–9, 203
Cezanne 52–3
Charnwood Forest 121
Chilly Billy 28, 30, 74
Cigar 160–1, 179
Classic Cliche 55, 82, 123, 153, 175
Commander in Chief 78, 123
Court of Honour 105–7, 123, 140, 155

Daffaq 78, 105, 108–10, 122
Dahlia 143, 190
Damister 32
Dancing Brave 46, 73, 96, 140, 159, 188
Danzig 32
Darley Arabian, The 11–13, 14, 15, 58, 184
Dayflower 53
Definite Article 124
Desert Orchid 17, 18, 65
Diomed 2, 14, 95, 97
Double Trigger 121

214